HOW TALL ARE THE TREES?

environmentally friendly book
100% recycled paper
care about the planet

When you see this symbol, ask an adult for help.

Forest Frolicks

How many animals are hiding in the forest?
Answer _____

A Change of Seasons

Draw a picture in each box to show how a forest would look in each season.

Spring

Summer

Autumn

Winter

5

Woodland Word Search

Circle these words in the puzzle.

ASPEN

BEECH

CHESTNUT

WILLOW

OAK

ELM

MAPLE

```
A S P E N U C B V M
I E A E G C H F R O
A M B A X R E L M P
G A W O T R S E U W
F P S A T F T A L I
B L T K W J N E K L
M E F L S P U A I L
N C O K O A T G M O
B E E C H Q Z L J W
T P K A D I N E G N
```

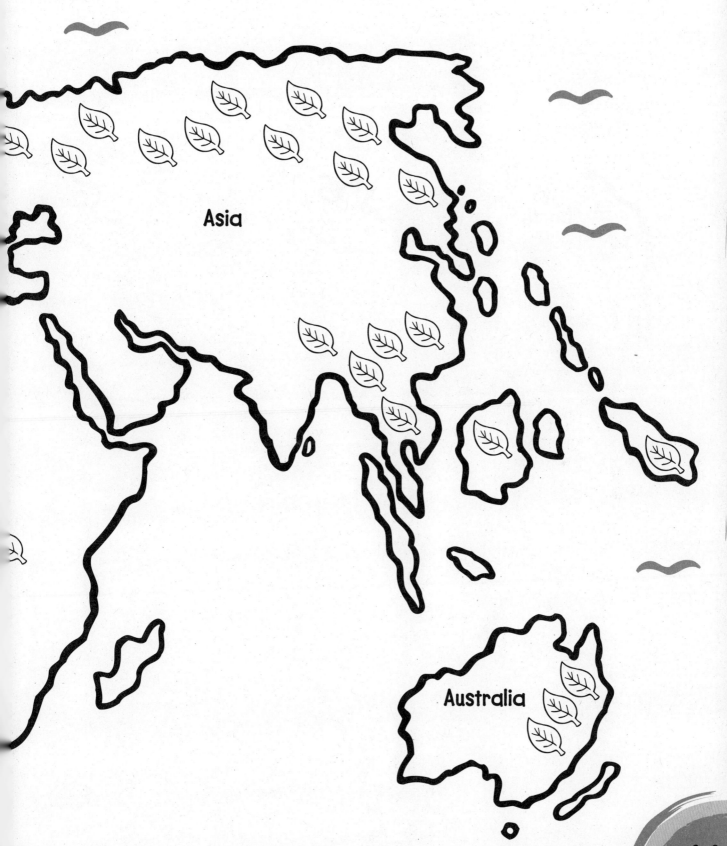

Asia

Australia

Number Problems

Complete the addition and subtraction problems.

14	−	6	=	
−	■	+	■	−
2	+		=	6
=	■	=	■	=
	−	10	=	2

18	−	2	=	16
−	■	+	■	−
4	+		=	6
=	■	=	■	=
	−	4	=	

12

Bonzai Bonanza

Color the picture.

Butterfly Art

Some butterflies have large 'eyes' on their wings to warn predators away. Draw eyes on this butterfly's wings. Color the picture.

Did you know that butterflies can see in virtually every direction at once?

A Trip to the Treetops

These animals spend most of their time in the treetops, where they find food and protection. Circle these words in the puzzle.

RED PANDA KOALA SLOTH
LEMUR MONKEY BUSHBABY
GIBBON AYE-AYE BAT

```
R  R  E  D  P  A  N  D  A
S  G  G  V  I  G  K  Q
L  Z  I  E  U  A  O  L
O  H  B  B  L  Z  A  E
T  S  B  A  X  E  L  M
H  A  O  T  L  Q  A  U
M  O  N  K  E  Y  N  R
Z  A  Y  E  A  Y  E  L
B  U  S  H  B  A  B  Y
```

Amazing Trees

The *Trembling Giant* in Utah is a colony of Quaking Aspen trees. It is composed of about 47,000 stems spread throughout 107 acres of land. It is estimated to weigh 6,600 tons, making it the heaviest known collective organism.

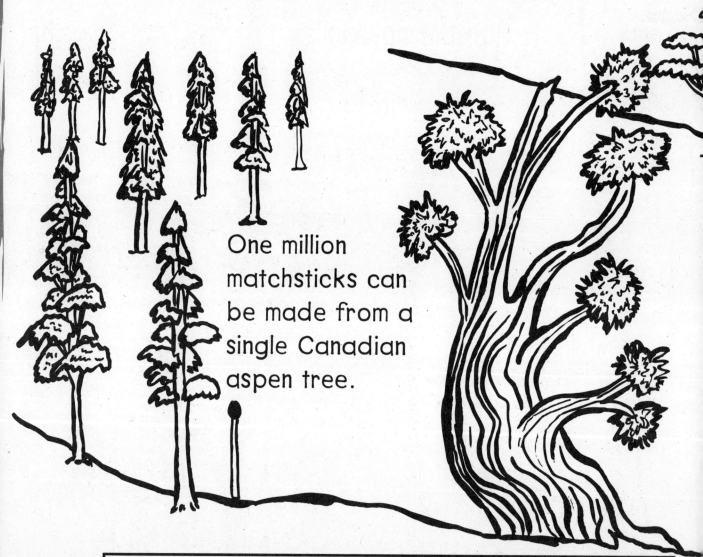

One million matchsticks can be made from a single Canadian aspen tree.

The world's oldest trees are bristlecone pines, located the USA. The oldest bristlecone pine is called the *Methuselah*, and is 4,835 years old. It still grows in the white mountains of California.

The world's largest giant sequoia is called *General Sherman.*
It has a height of about 275 ft. (84 m) and a girth of 25 ft. (7 m).

There are about 20,000 tree species in the world.

The trunk of a baobab is fire resistant, and its bark is used to make cloth and rope.

Lizard Lunch

Color the picture.

Copy Cat!

Draw the gorilla in the grid.

Seasons Change

Draw a picture in each box to show the weather for each season.

Spring

Summer

Autumn

Winter

Word Scramble

Unscramble the letters to reveal two words.
The picture is a clue.

eeMrnekyoT

_ _ _ _ _ _ _ _ _

_ _ _ _ _

Lots of Legs

The name millipede comes from the Latin root meaning "a thousand legs", but millipedes rarely have more than 200–300 legs.

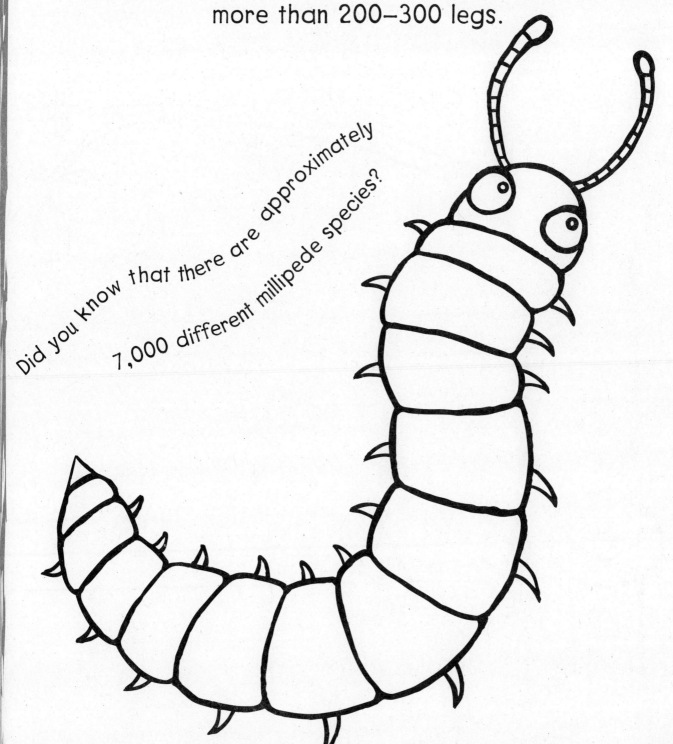

Did you know that there are approximately 7,000 different millipede species?

How many legs does this millipede have?

_____

New Zealand Birds

How many birds can you find in this picture?____

Did you know that New Zealand kakapos are the only parrots that cannot fly? Fewer than 100 kakapos exist in the wild.

Circus Trees

Farmer Axel Erlandson trained trees to form amazing shapes, such as ladders and arches. He called them *Circus Trees*. Draw your own circus tree.

Did you know that Axel Erlandson never shared his secret for creating such strangely-shaped trees?

Worms Away

How many worms can you find in this picture? _____

Did you know that the earthworm's biggest enemy is the mole, who eats 50 worms each day?

Fun Facts

The jewel beetle is known for

    a. its iridescent colors
    b. its size
    c. its legs

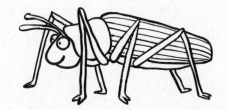

Trivia Time

Dendrochronology is the study of

    a. tree-ring dating
    b. smelling eggs
    c. washing dishes

Honey to the Bee

Moving left to right, use the letters in the order they are given to form a sentence.

Th edi sapp eara nceo fbe esi ntheUSi samy stery

___ ___ ___ ___ ___ ___ ___ ___ ___

___ ___ ___ ___ ___ ___ ___ ___

___ . ___ . ___ ___ ___ ___ ___ ___ .

Did you know that honey bees communicate with each other by dancing?

Draw More

Complete this picture.

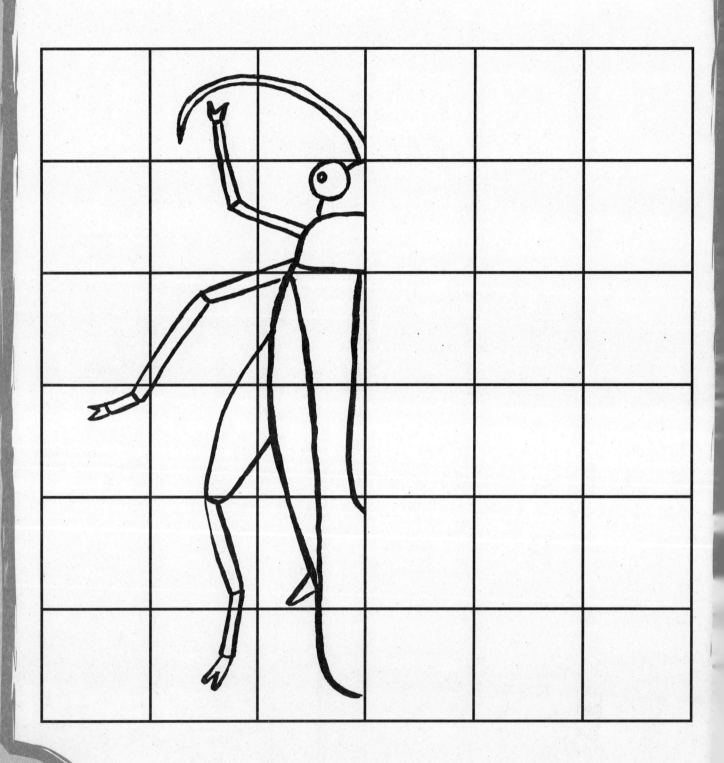

Slithering Snakes

Circle these words in the puzzle.

PYTHON ANACONDA MAMBA ADDER
COBRA BOA RATTLE CORN

```
S  A  D  D  E  R  B  A
P  P  C  F  M  P  O  N
O  B  S  U  A  E  A  A
P  A  R  N  M  H  E  C
Y  B  A  G  B  E  C  O
Y  T  T  S  A  E  C  N
H  N  T  F  R  N  O  D
O  W  L  C  O  B  R  A
N  M  E  O  R  M  N  K
```

The Tree of Life

In Morocco, the *argan tree* is known as the *tree of life* because it helps many creatures survive in the semi-arid southern desert.

How many goats are in this tree? _____

Did you know that goats can climb trees to find food?

Pretty Flowers

Which flower is different?

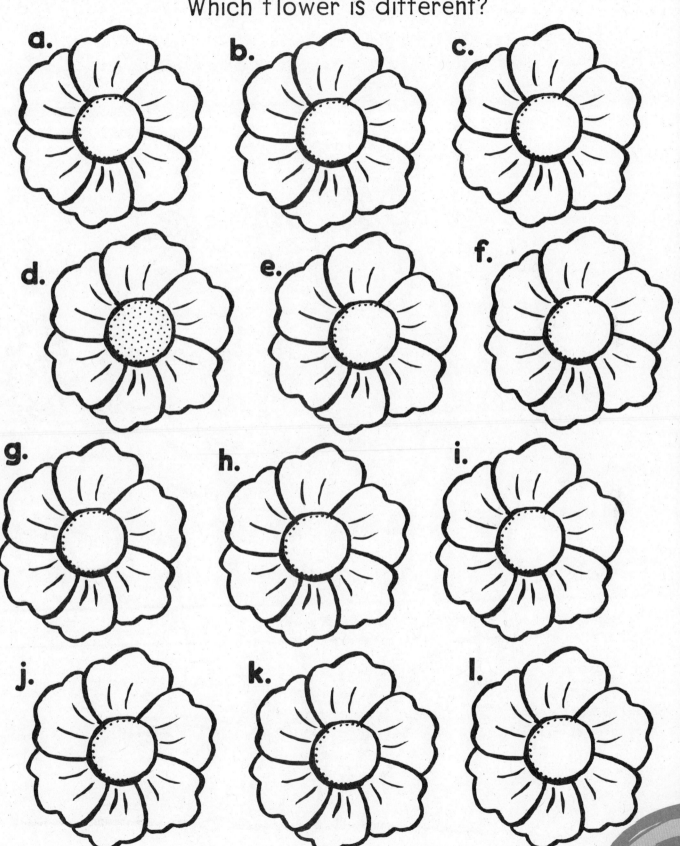

Lost!

Draw a line to help the explorer
find his way out of the jungle.

Start

Finish

What Am I?

Use the clues to discover the name of an insect.

My first letter is in **farm,** but not in **arm**.

My second letter is in **lake,** but not in **take**.

My third letter is in **yellow,** but not in **fellow**.

I am a _ _ _ .

Amazing Amazon

One-fifth of the world's fresh water comes from the Amazon, the world's largest tropical rain forest.

The Amazon is home to some of the world's most unusual wildlife.

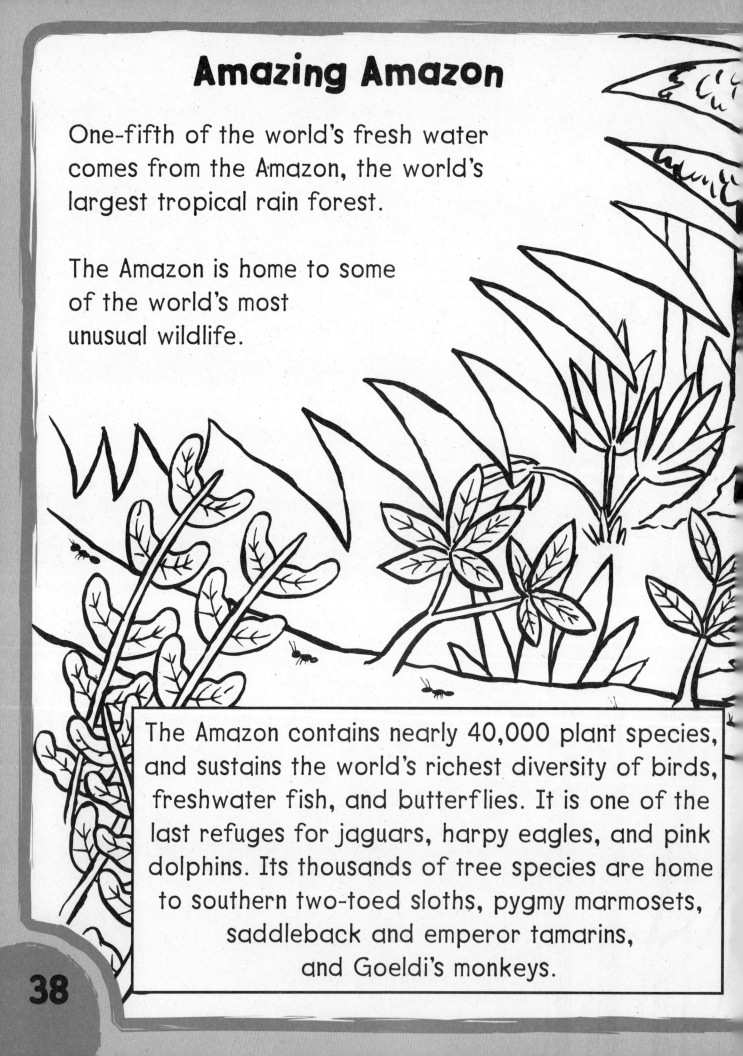

The Amazon contains nearly 40,000 plant species, and sustains the world's richest diversity of birds, freshwater fish, and butterflies. It is one of the last refuges for jaguars, harpy eagles, and pink dolphins. Its thousands of tree species are home to southern two-toed sloths, pygmy marmosets, saddleback and emperor tamarins, and Goeldi's monkeys.

The Amazon's vegetation represents about one-third of the remaining forests on Earth, and provides about 15% of the world's oxygen. The Amazon River is 3,902 miles (6,280 km) long, making it the second longest river in the world.

Trivia Time

What is the name of the tallest giant sequoia?

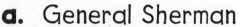

a. General Sherman
b. Lieutenant Sherman
c. Colonel Sherman
d. Private Sherman

Bird Watch

Circle these words in the puzzle.

dove

finch

parrot

albatross

canary

eagle

H	K	M	M	I	N	P	A
B	I	T	D	F	G	A	L
R	D	P	P	I	G	R	B
A	O	O	E	N	T	R	A
Y	V	K	L	C	A	O	T
D	E	U	E	H	O	T	R
E	O	R	I	N	C	H	O
L	Z	E	A	G	L	E	S
C	A	N	A	R	Y	P	S

41

Flower Time

How many flowers can you find in this scene?

43

Life Under Leaf

Fill in the blanks with the words below.

canopy

plant

animal

forest

In the rainforest, most _ _ _ _ _ and _ _ _ _ _ _ life is not found on the _ _ _ _ _ _ floor, but in the leafy world known as the canopy. The _ _ _ _ _ _, which may be more than 100 feet above the ground, is made of the overlapping branches and _ _ _ _ _ _ in the _ _ _ _ _.

trees

leaves

44

Rhyme Time

How many words can you think of that rhyme with *tree*?
Write your answers in the tree.

Somewhere in North America

Match the numbers on the map back to the pictures to discover what trees grow where.

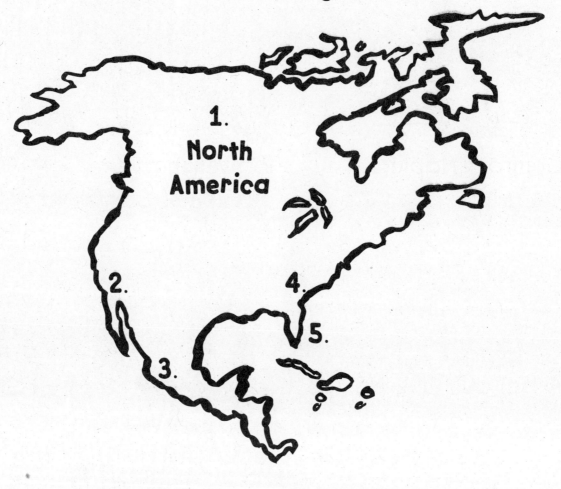

1. North America

2.

3.

4.

5.

4. The Angel Oak, South Carolina

1. Comfort Maple,
   Ontario

2. Avenue of the
   Giants, California

3. Arbol del Tule, Mexico

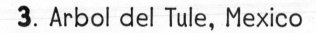

5. The Edison Ford
   Banyan Tree,
   Florida

Tree Word Search

Circle these words in the puzzle.

ACORN   BARK   BUDS   FIR

FRUIT   LEAVES

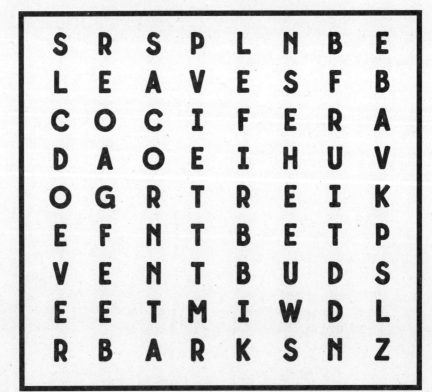

S R S P L N B E
L E A V E S F B
C O C I F E R A
D A O E I H U V
O G R T R E I K
E F N T B E T P
V E N T B U D S
E E T M I W D L
R R B A R K S N Z

Did you know that bark protects a tree against external threats, such as bad weather and animals?

What's Hiding?

Many of the largest rain forest animals live on the forest floor. Connect the dots from 1-22. Start at 1.

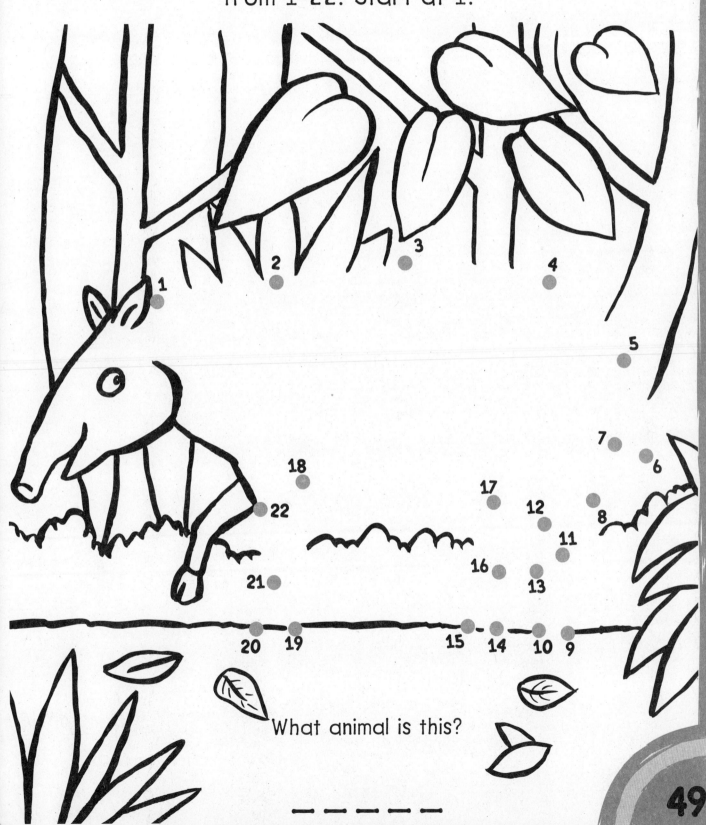

What animal is this?

_ _ _ _ _ _

Kind Koala

Color the picture.

Letter First

Write the first letter of each picture in the middle of the circle. Unscramble the letters to spell the name of an animal that swings from the trees.

____ ____ ____ ____ ____

Copy Cat!

Draw the owl in the grid.

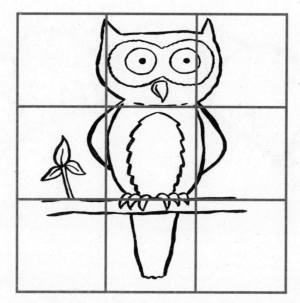

How Many?

How many different types of flowers can you think of?
Write their names in the middle of this flower.

Picking Fruit

Circle these words in the puzzle.

cherry

apple

plum

fig

pear

orange

```
M P Z P B N O E
L L A V E S R B
C U C I F E A A
H M H E I H N V
E I G H G E G K
R M N T O R E P
R P E A R R O M
Y E T M I W R L
R R A P P L E N Y
```

Where Is It From?

Which of these foods is not made from a plant?

coffee

tea

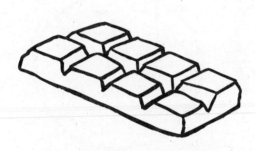

chocolate

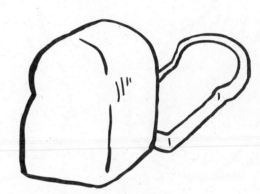

bread

cheese

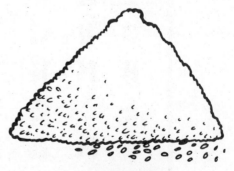

rice

Did you know that there are 30,000 edible plants in the world?

The Bees and the Birds

Insects are attracted to a flower's sweet smell,
bright appearance, and sugary nectar.
Color these flowers to attract the bees.

To produce seeds, flowers must be pollinated. Insects and birds often transfer pollen when looking for nectar. Draw more bees to pollinate these flowers.

Dot to Dot

Connect the dots from 1-25. Start at 1
to reveal the fastest flying insect.

8

9

7

5

10

4

11

6

3

12

2   1   13

25

14

24   15

16

19   18

17

23   20

22   21

Who's Sneaking around the Garden?

Color the picture.

59

Songbirds

Fit these songbirds into the crossword puzzle.
Some letters have been done for you.

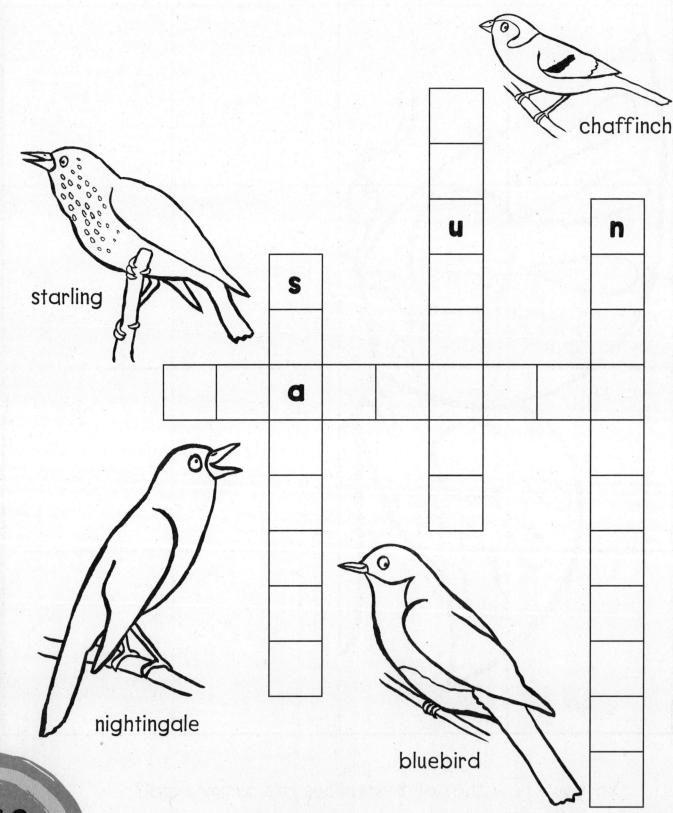

chaffinch

starling

nightingale

bluebird

Copy Cat!

Complete this picture.

Did you know that all butterflies are symmetrical?

Deforestation

At the current rate of deforestation, the world's rain forests could completely vanish in 100 years.

Forests are home to 70% of Earth's plants and land animals. Many of them cannot survive the deforestation that destroys their homes.

Rapid deforestation threatens the Amazon. At current rates, 55% of its rain forests could be gone by 2030.

Without trees, many forest lands can quickly become barren deserts.

Power plants and other industries cut and burn trees to generate electricity.

The paper industry turns huge tracts of rain forest trees into pulp.

At the current rate of tropical forest loss, 5–10% of tropical rain forest species will be lost each decade.

Trivia Time

Which of these animals cannot climb trees?

a. goat
b. monkey
c. leopard
d. bear

Types of Trees

Circle these words in the puzzle.

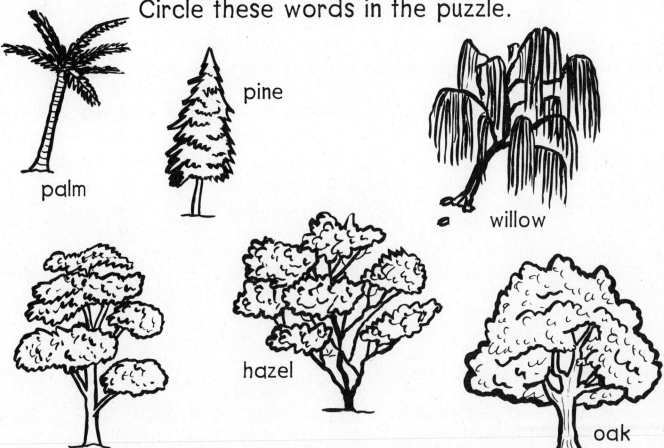

palm

pine

willow

sycamore

hazel

oak

A	H	P	L	E	N	S	E
H	A	A	V	P	S	Y	B
C	Z	C	I	A	E	C	A
D	E	Z	E	L	H	A	V
O	L	R	E	M	E	M	K
P	G	W	I	L	L	O	W
I	P	E	J	R	R	R	M
N	L	T	M	I	W	E	L
E	N	A	C	O	A	K	Y

Number Problems

Complete the addition and subtraction problems.

8	+		=	10
+	■	−	■	+
8	−	2	=	
=	■	=	■	=
	+	0	=	

	+	2	=	
+	■	−	■	+
9	−		=	7
=	■	=	■	=
11	+	0	=	

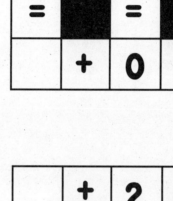

Find the Difference

Circle the differences in the pictures.

Number Word Search

Complete the addition and subtraction problems.
Circle the answers in the word search.

5 + 10 = ☐

10 + 30 = ☐

☐ + 3 = 13

12 - 3 = ☐

8 - ☐ = 4

15 - 1 = ☐

```
A X P L E N S E
S F O U R S Y B
C O C I A E F A
D U Z E L H I V
O R R E M E F K
P T W F O R T Y
T E N A R R E M
F E T N I N E L
E N A C O A N Y
```

Find the Difference

Circle the differences in the pictures.

69

In the Woods

Color the picture.

70

Busy Bees

1. Where a bee gets nectar
2. What bees collect to make honey
3. A male bee
4. Sugary liquid that bees drink from flowers
5. Bees produce this

Buggy Key

Use this key to solve the secret message.

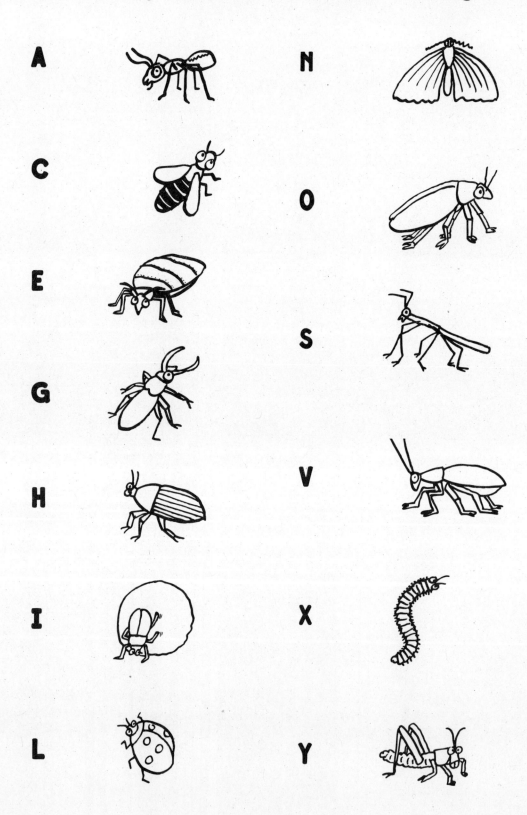

A

C

E

G

H

I

L

N

O

S

V

X

Y

"

___ ___ ___ ___ ___ ___ ___

___ ___ ___ ___ ___ ___ ___ .

___ ___ ___ ___ ___ .

"

___ ___ ___ ___ ___ .

Which insect is saying this?

An ___ ___ ___

Where on Earth?

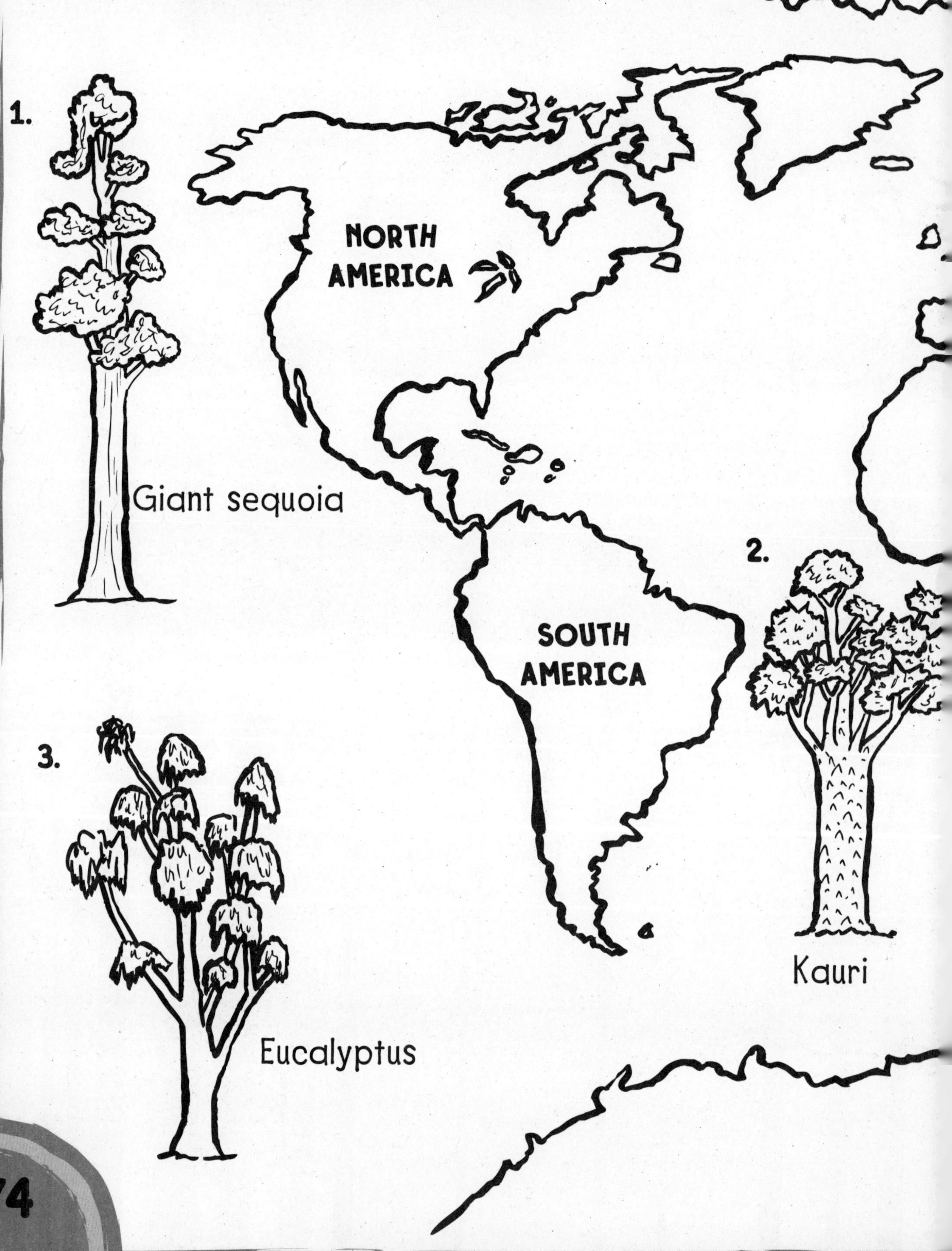

1.

Giant sequoia

NORTH
AMERICA

SOUTH
AMERICA

2.

Kauri

3.

Eucalyptus

Draw a line to match each tree with its native continent or country.

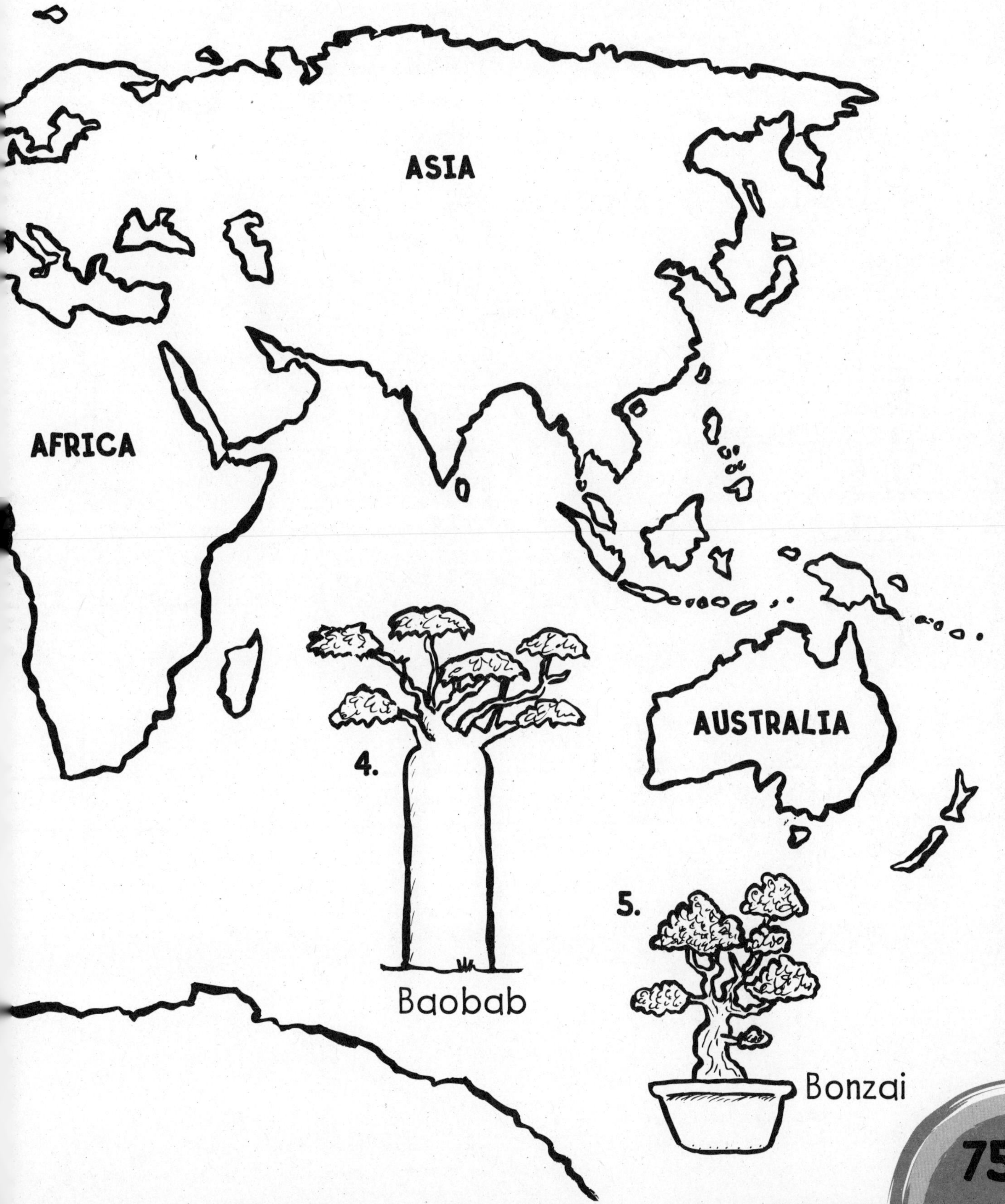

ASIA

AFRICA

AUSTRALIA

4.

Baobab

5.

Bonzai

What Am I?

I am long and thin.
I sway in the breeze.
I am easily mistaken for a stick.

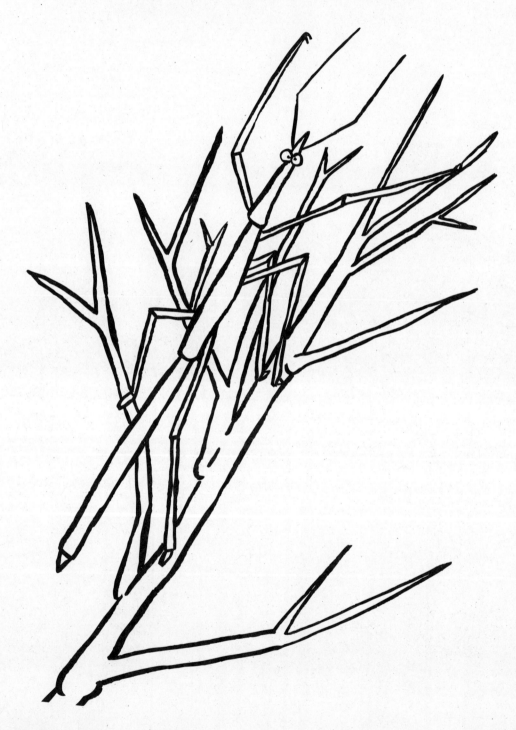

I am a _____ _____ .

Bird Watching

In your backyard or local park,
see how many different bird species you can find.
Try to identify them. Draw a picture of each one.

Trivia Time

How old is the world's oldest tree?

a. Between 10 and 15 years old

b. Between 145 and 200 years old

c. Between 4,700 and 4,774 years old

d. Over 9,000 years old

Make-and-Do Leaf Rubbing

You will need:
Crayon Scissors Paper Glue Leaves

Leaves come in many shapes and sizes—long
and narrow, round and spikey. Find two different leaves.
Put a piece of paper over each leaf, then gently rub
a crayon over the paper—an image should appear!

Ask an adult to help you cut out your leaf rubbings
and glue them in the boxes below. Do you know the name
of each leaf? Write their names below each box with the
details of where you found them.

Horsing Around

Color the picture.

Make-and-Do Butterfly Handprint

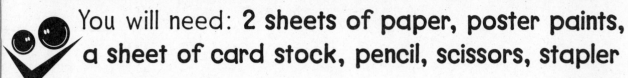

You will need: **2 sheets of paper, poster paints, a sheet of card stock, pencil, scissors, stapler**

1. Dip one hand into the poster paint. Make sure the paint is thinly spread, and covers your entire hand.

2. Carefully place your hand on the paper, making sure your entire hand touches the paper. Lift your hand, taking care not to smudge the image.

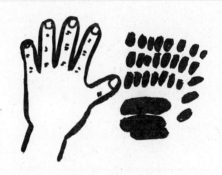

3. Move your hand slightly each time, until you have several overlapping handprints. Repeat this process with your other hand.

4. Draw your butterfly a body on card stock—don't forget to draw antennae.

5. Once the paint is dry, ask an adult to help you cut around the handprints so that the butterfly has frilled wings. Staple the handprints to the body.

In the Desert

Cacti have adapted to grow in places, such as deserts, where there is not much water.

Deserts get very little rain, are very hot during the daytime, and often frosty at night.

The Gila woodpecker nests inside the stem of the saguaro cactus, where the temperature inside can be up to 86°F (30°C) cooler than outside.

The tallest cactus species in the world is the giant saguaro, growing up to 67 ft. (20 m) high. It can weigh up to six tons.

Cactus needles prevent birds and animals from drinking water from the cactus.

Some cacti can live up to 250 years.

Sometimes, in the desert, it doesn't rain for months. Some cacti have swollen roots that store water for days when it doesn't rain.

All Mixed-Up

Can you identify all of the animals and insects shown below? What would you call this odd creature?

How Many?

How many dragonflies can you find? ____

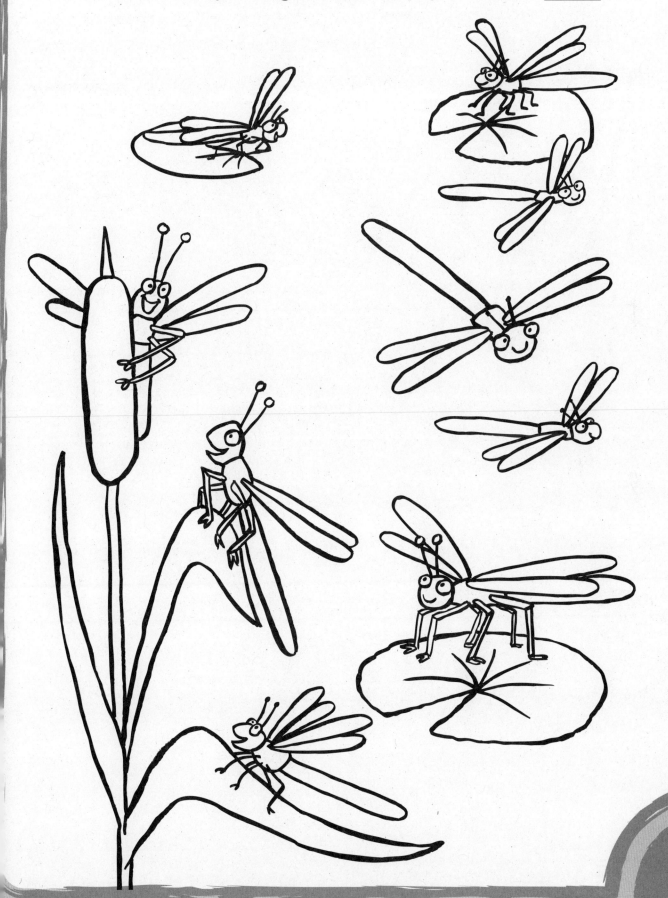

Rain Forest Find

Many countries have rain forests. Unscramble these words to find which countries have the most rain forests.

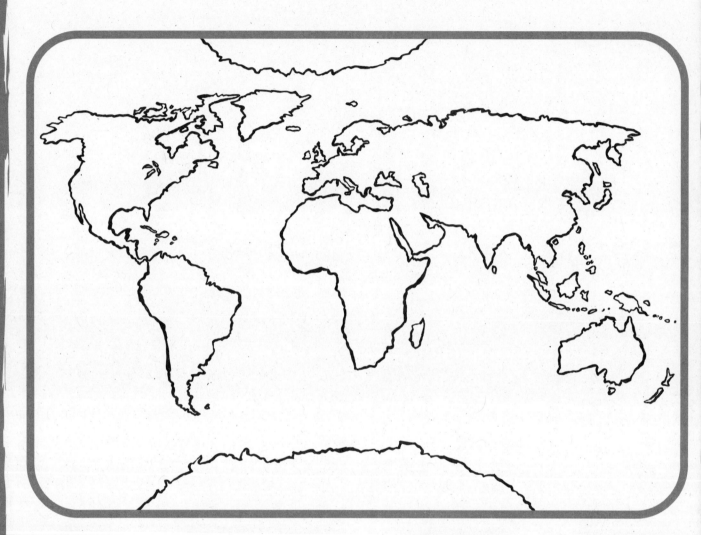

raBzli   **donInsiae**   **olBiiav**   **goCno**

ngAloa   **Veneleuza**

aPapu ewN uinGea   **exMico**   **ndIai**

_____

_____

Trivia Time

Some damselfly nymphs shed and regrow their skin. How many times on average does this happen before adulthood?

a. once
b. 20 times
c. 100 times

Which insect can grow up to 20 in. (50 cm) long?

a. stick bug
b. stag beetle
c. butterfly

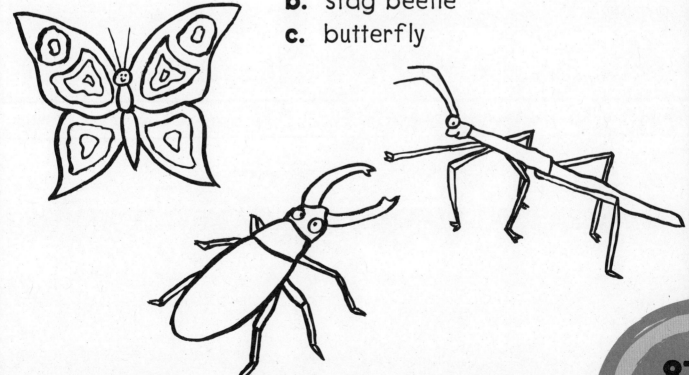

Canopy Capers

Draw a line to help the scientist find her way to the canopy.

Finish

Start

All About Trees

Circle these words in the puzzle.

NUTS   OAK   PINECONE   RINGS

SAP   TIMBER   TRUNK

M	P	H	L	E	N	S	E
R	I	N	G	S	S	Y	B
C	N	T	I	M	B	E	R
D	E	Z	G	P	H	A	V
O	C	R	E	B	E	M	K
P	O	N	I	Z	T	O	W
S	N	U	A	R	R	S	M
A	E	T	R	U	N	K	L
P	N	S	S	O	A	K	Y

Bugs About

How many of each insect can you find in this picture?

Write the answers in each box.

Toucan Tricks

Color the picture.

What Am I?

My first letter is in **gate**, but not in **mate**.

My second letter is in **road**, but not in **load**.

My third letter is in **run**, but not in **ran**.

My last letter is in **boat**, but not in **coat**.

I am a __ __ __ __ .

Make-and-Do Birdy Breakfast

Help feed the birds in your backyard
by making this nutritious treat.
You will need:

**An empty coconut shell (or alternate item),
suet, 1/2 cup mixed seeds,
1/4 cup raisins, and string**

1. Ask an adult to help make a hole in one side of the coconut shell and tie the string through the hole.

2. Ask an adult to help you melt the suet over low heat. When melted, remove the suet from the heat and mix it in a bowl with the raisins and seeds.

3. Scoop the mixture into the coconut shell and chill in the refrigerator.

4. Hang the bird feeder on a branch, then watch the birds gather.

Pond Life

1. Warty relative of the frog
2. This unwanted plant can take over a pond
3. A pretty water flower
4. A type of fly named after a fire-breathing monster
5. This creature becomes a frog

95

A Matter of Survival

Unscramble these words to find the names of parts of a tree, and what trees need to survive.

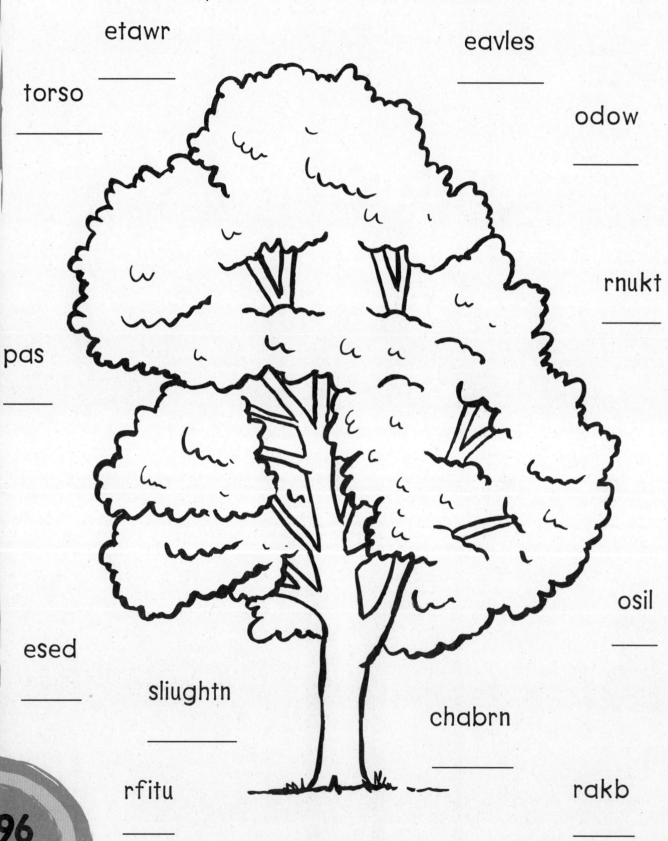

etawr
_____

torso
_____

eavles
_____

odow
_____

rnukt
_____

pas
_____

esed
_____

sliughtn
_____

osil
_____

chabrn
_____

rfitu
_____

rakb
_____

Autumn Leaves

Color the picture.

Rain Forests

Covering less than 2% of Earth's total surface area, rain forests are home to 50% of Earth's plants and animals.

A typical four square mile area of rain forest contains as many as 1,500 species of flowering plants, 750 species of trees, 400 species of birds, and 150 species of butterflies.

More than 56,000 sq. miles (145,040 sq. km) of natural forests are lost annually.

Rain forests provide many important products for people, including timber, coffee, cocoa, and many medicinal products.

Hanging Around

Color the picture.

Number Problems

Complete the addition and subtraction problems.

	+	9	=	13
+	■	−	■	+
10	−		=	7
=	■	=	■	=
14	+	6	=	

	+	11	=	16
+	■	+	■	+
6	+		=	9
=	■	=	■	=
11	+	14	=	

Letter Wheel

Write the first letter of each animal name beside each picture in the wheel to spell something that grows on trees.

__ __ __ __

Parrot Party

Fit these words into the crossword grid.
Some letters have been done for you.

macaw

o

e

w

c

e

i

t

cockatoo

lorikeet

kea

budgerigar

Primates Puzzler

Circle these words in the puzzle.

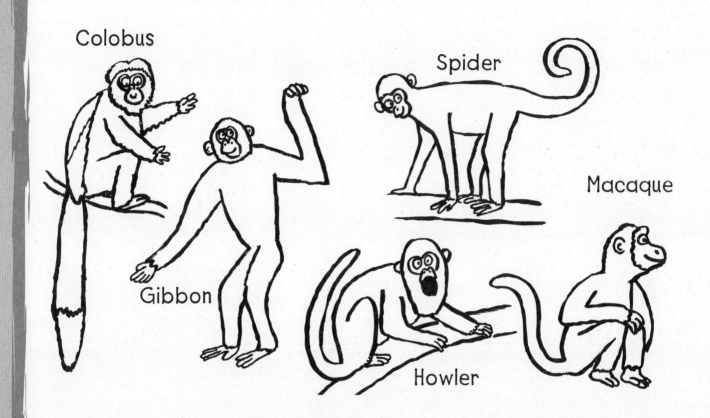

Colobus

Spider

Macaque

Gibbon

Howler

```
S  P  H  L  E  N  S  E
P  H  O  W  L  E  R  R
I  N  W  I  M  B  E  M
D  G  Z  L  P  H  A  A
E  I  R  E  X  E  M  C
R  B  W  I  Z  R  O  A
S  B  A  C  L  P  E  Q
C  O  L  O  B  U  S  U
P  N  A  C  Z  U  E  E
```

Make-and-Do Fabulous Flowers

With an adult's permission, pick three flowers from your yard. Put a piece of paper on either side of the flowers and place them into the middle of a heavy book. Close the book and put another heavy book on top for a few weeks.

Carefully remove the pressed flowers from the book. You can use them to make a greeting card or a collage.

Which Wasp?

Which wasp does not belong?

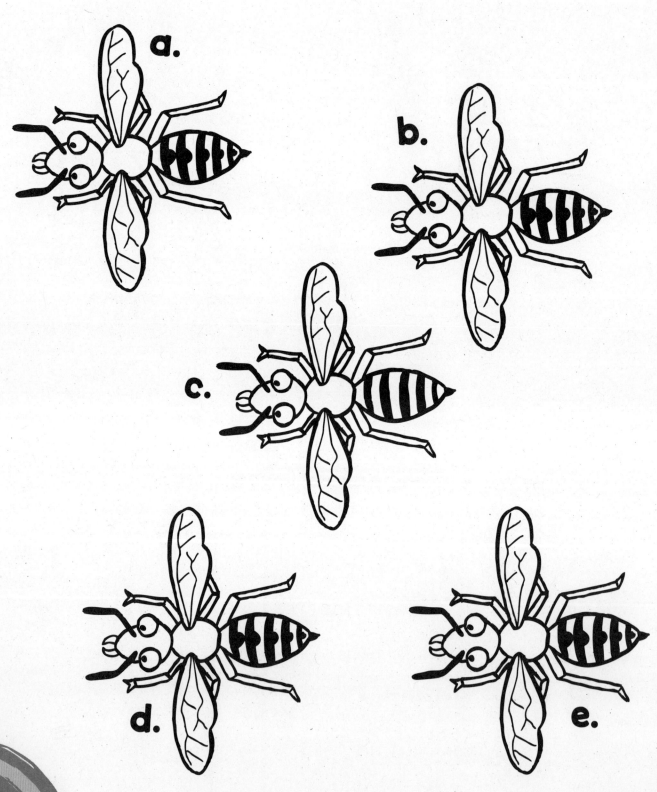

Monkey Business

Which monkey does not belong?

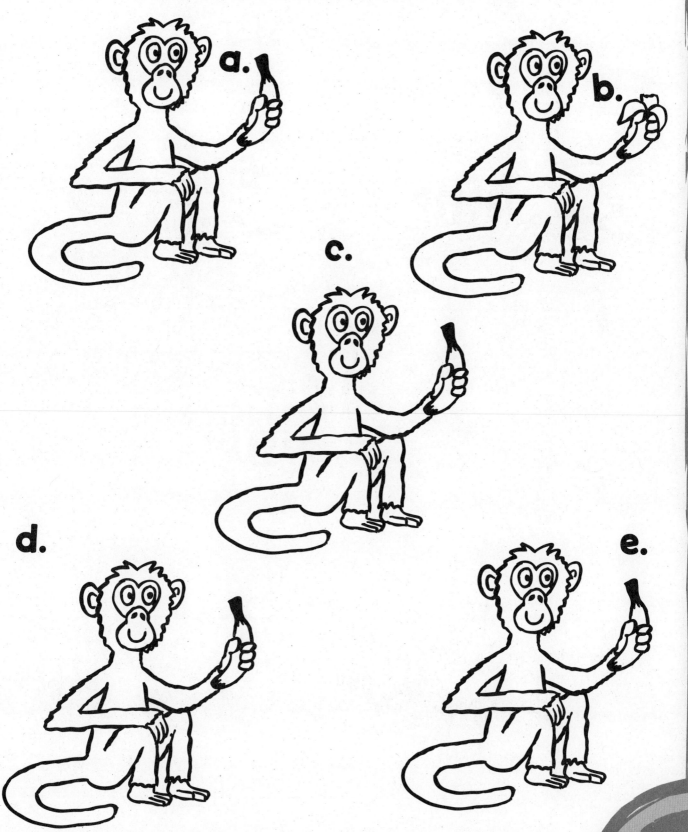

A Day in the Life

Tree rings provide information about a tree's age.
How old are these trees?

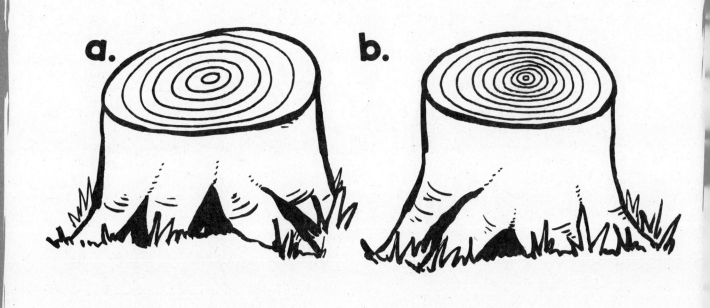

a.

_____

b.

_____

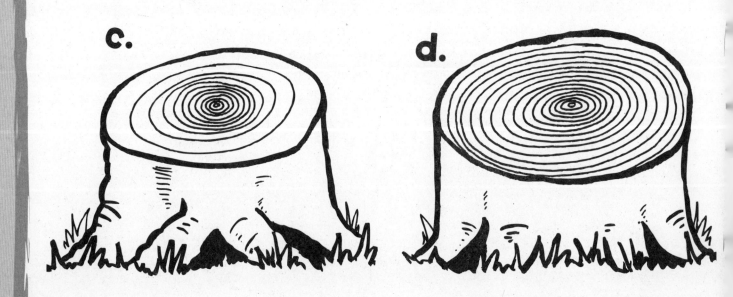

c.

_____

d.

_____

Find the Difference

Circle the differences in the pictures.

Flamingo Fun
Color the picture.

Ant Antics

Ants leave a scent trail to guide each other to food.
Help the ant follow the correct scent trail to find the food.

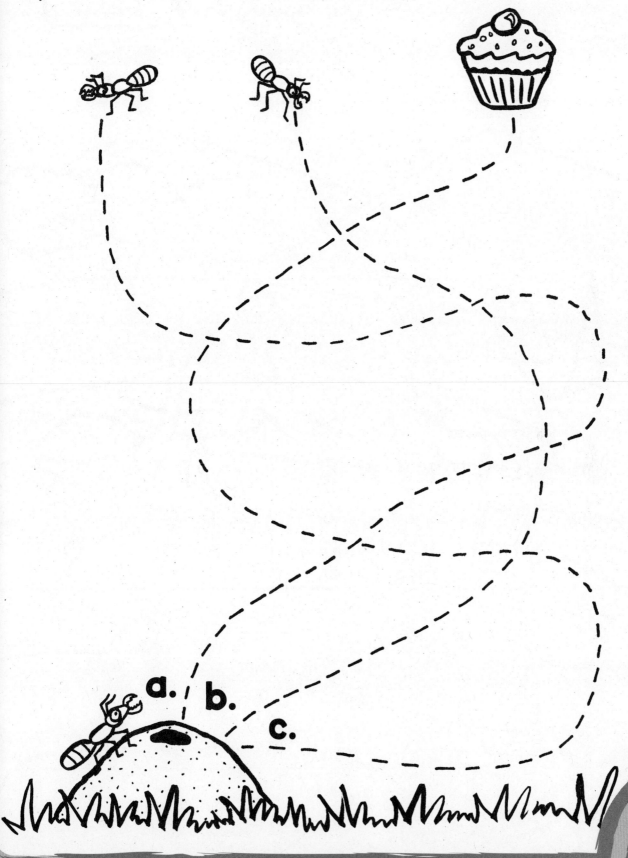

Rain Forest Birds

Place the names of these rain forest birds into the puzzle.
Some letters have been done for you.

CASSOWARY   MACAW   TOUCAN

LORIKEET   HORNBILL

Leafy Business

Circle the matching pair of leaves.

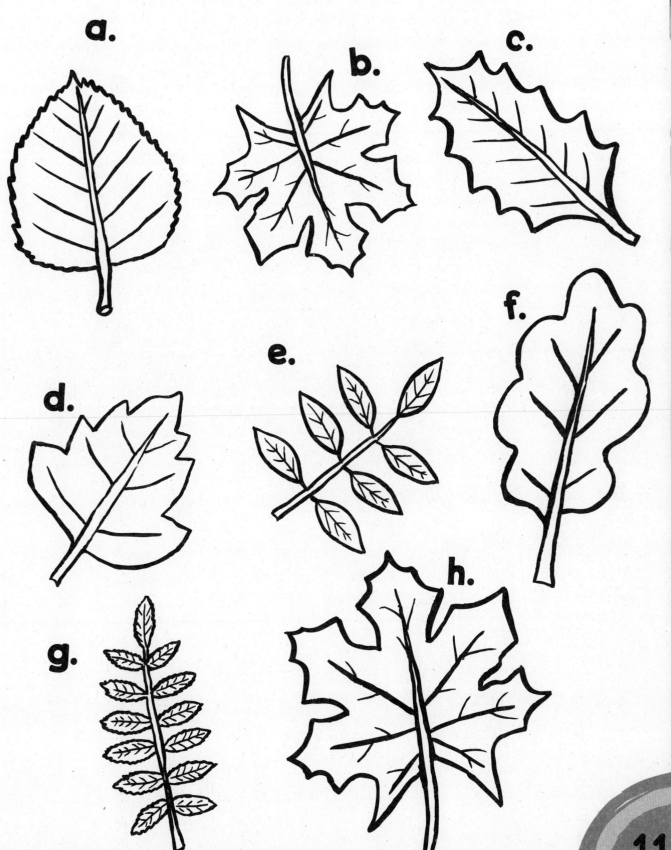

a.

b.

c.

d.

e.

f.

g.

h.

Make-and-Do Caterpillar

Caterpillars can be every shade of the rainbow, and covered in spots and stripes. Make your own bright, recycled caterpillar.

You will need:

1 egg carton, yarn, scissors, poster paints, tape, a straw, glue, and 2 buttons or googly eyes

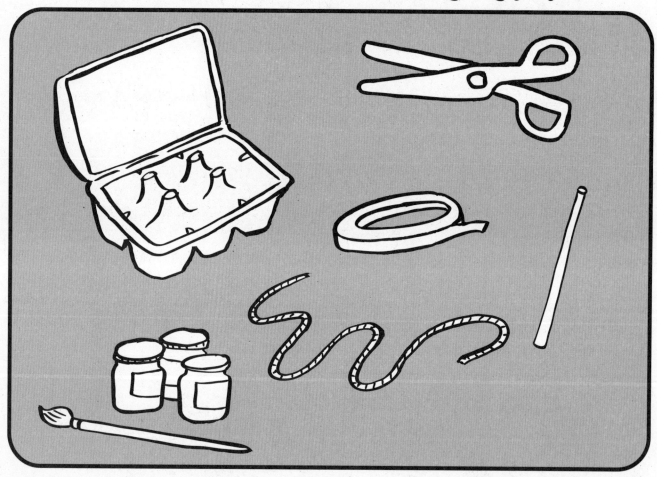

1. Cut out each segment of the egg carton.

2. Poke one hole in either side of each cup.

3. Pull the yarn through each hole and fasten with tape on the inside of each segment. Tie a knot on each end.

4. Paint your caterpillar and add spots, stripes, and wiggly lines. Let the paint dry.

5. To make feelers, cut two equal-sized pieces of straw. Poke two holes on the top of the head, and push each straw into the holes.

6. To add eyes, glue two small buttons or googly eyes to the face.

7. Cut a small piece of yarn and glue it to the caterpillar's face to make a smile.

All Mixed-Up

Can you identify all of the insects shown below?
What would you call this odd bug?

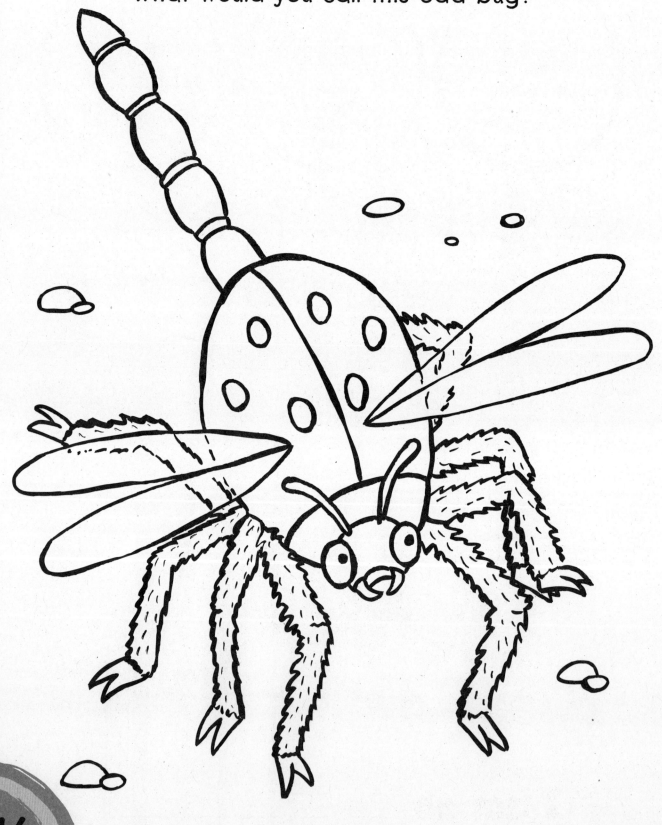

What Am I?

I grow on some trees.

I am a seed.

Squirrels gather me for winter.

I am an ＿ ＿ ＿ ＿ ＿ ＿ .

Butterfly Beginnings

Complete each picture.

Farmyard Frolics

Color the picture.

Spider Speller

How many words can you make from *Sally Spider*?
Write the answers inside the spider's body.

SALLY SPIDER

Interesting Insects

In a beehive, there may be as many as 80,000 worker bees who build the colony and gather food.

A bee will perform a special dance to point the way to the location of a rich nectar source.

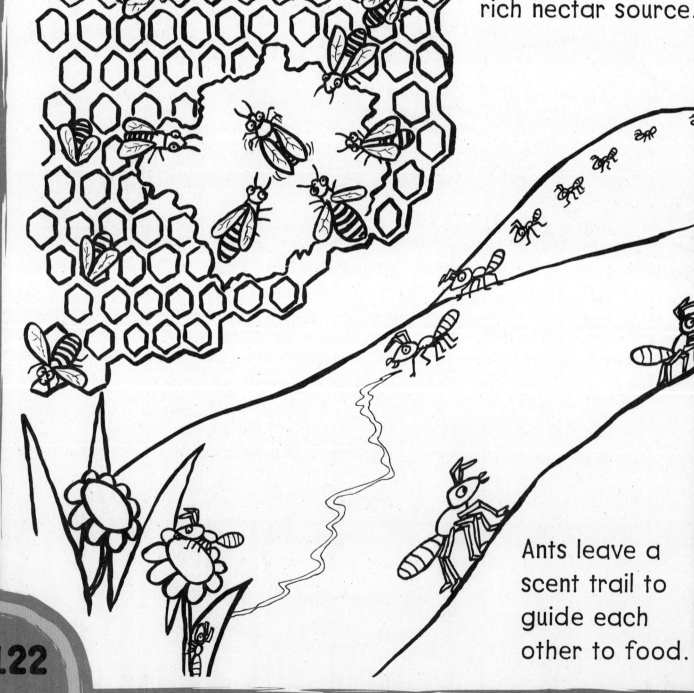

Ants leave a scent trail to guide each other to food.

A queen termite may lay 30,000 eggs in one day, and there may be up to 7 million termites in a colony.

Worker termites make a collective hiss when they hear an animal approach, making the predator believe a snake is nearby.

If attacked, some termites will blow themselves apart, covering their attackers in slime to prevent them from reaching the colony.

Secret Message

Moving left to right, use the letters in the order they are given to form a sentence.

Pre ttyp ollyw ant sac rack er

" _ _ _ _ _ _ _

_ _ _ _ _

_ _ _ _ _ . "

Spots of Fun

Decorate these ladybugs with spots.

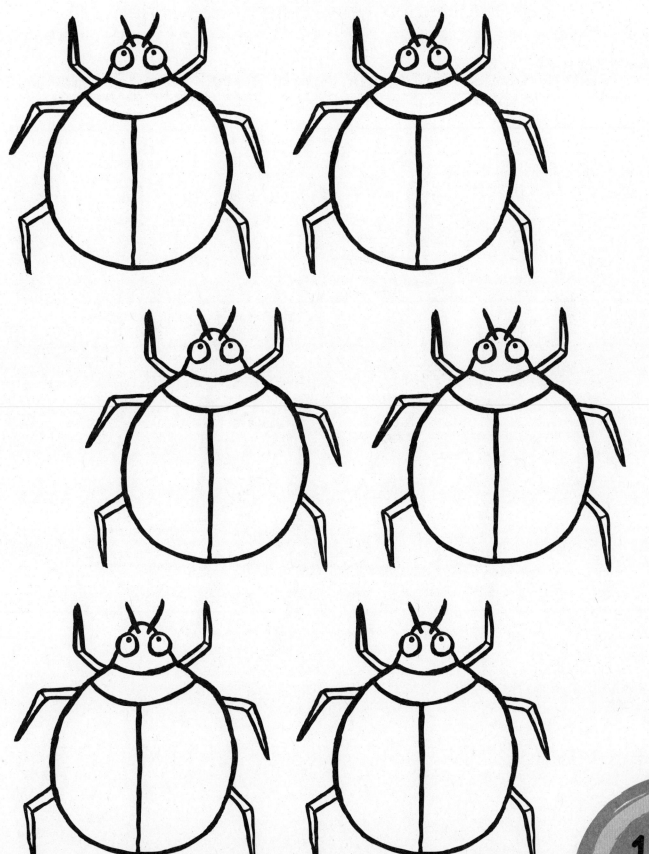

Number Word Search

Complete the addition and subtraction problems.
Circle the number words in the word search.

4 + 4 = ☐

7 + 4 = ☐

8 + ☐ = 10

10 − 3 = ☐

2 + ☐ = 7

15 − 3 = ☐

```
B  L  P  L  E  T  S  E
S  F  I  V  E  W  Y  B
C  O  H  I  A  E  F  A
D  U  Z  E  L  L  I  V
O  S  R  E  M  V  F  T
Q  E  L  E  V  E  N  W
I  V  T  A  R  R  E  O
F  E  I  G  H  T  E  L
E  N  A  C  O  A  N  Y
```

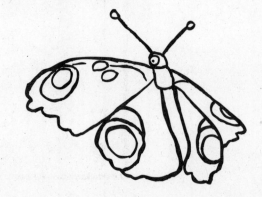

Creepy Crawlies

Circle these words in the puzzle.

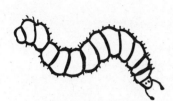

millipede

snail

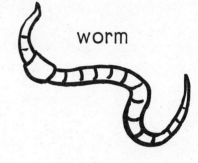

worm

bee

wasp

fly

H	P	H	L	E	N	M	E
S	N	A	I	L	C	I	R
C	N	W	I	M	X	L	J
D	G	Z	L	P	A	L	A
W	O	R	M	E	O	I	C
P	J	N	W	Z	R	P	F
F	L	Y	A	L	P	E	U
C	O	L	S	P	G	D	E
P	N	A	P	B	E	E	S

What Doesn't Belong?

Which one of these centipedes does not belong?

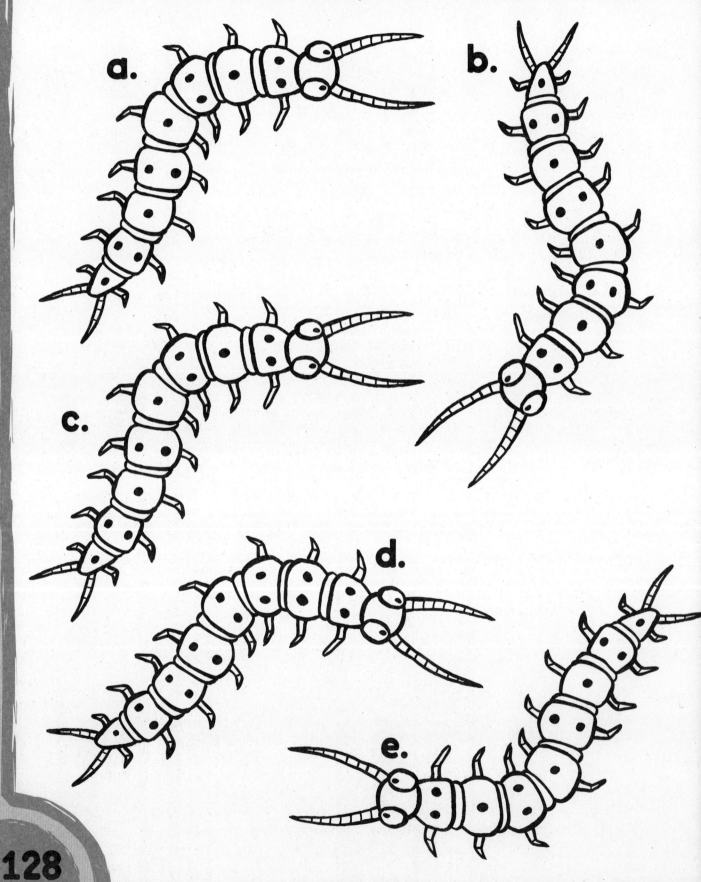

a.

b.

c.

d.

e.

Trivia Time

Which insect has 100 legs?

a. millipede **b.** centipede **c.** woodlouse

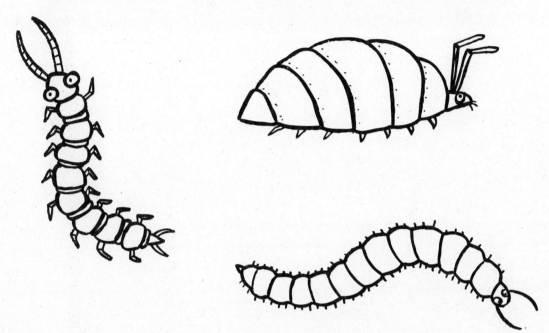

How wide is the largest cicada's wingspan?

a. 0.8 in. (2 cm) **b.** 4 in. (10 cm) **c.** 6 in. (15 cm)

Anteater Antics

Color the picture.

130

Make-and-Do Pet Rocks

What you will need:
Poster paint, paintbrush, googly eyes, and different-shaped rocks

1. Find some interesting shaped rocks.

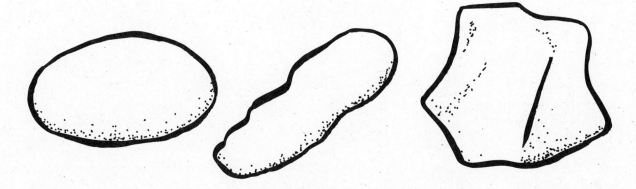

2. Clean the rocks, and use poster paint to create different bugs or animals.

3. Add a pair of googly eyes to complete your rock pet.

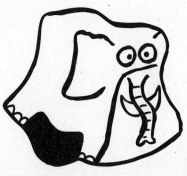

Beehive Buzz

A single hive contains up to 50,000 bees.

How many bees can you spot in this picture?

_____

What Am I?

My first letter is in **wing,** but not in **king.**
My second letter is in **pale,** but not in **peel.**
My third letter is in **sugar,** and also in **spice.**
My last letter is in **pace,** but not in **face.**

I am a ___ ___ ___ ___ .

Cacti Coloring

Color this picture.

135

Counting Acorns

A fully-grown oak sheds about 250,000 leaves
and produces around 50,000 acorns in a good year.

How many acorns can you find in this picture?

_____

Tree Museums

A place where trees are grown for science
and education is called an

a. arboretum
b. jungle
c. tree land

Word Search

Circle these words in the puzzle.

TARANTULA   **BLACK WIDOW**   **WOLF**

WEB   **MONEY**   **PURSE**

H	P	T	L	E	N	M	E	C	V
B	L	A	C	K	W	I	D	O	W
P	N	R	W	I	O	E	Q	L	D
U	G	A	E	M	L	K	X	V	Z
R	E	N	B	P	F	L	L	O	X
S	B	T	W	B	R	S	F	N	P
E	L	U	A	S	P	I	G	E	R
C	O	L	L	S	E	D	E	B	H
P	M	A	M	O	N	E	Y	S	P

Did you know that spider silk is only about
1/200th mm in diameter?

Wise Owl

Color the picture.

In the Treetops

Color the picture.

Missing Letters

Complete these words.

_guana

_corpion

_ragonfly

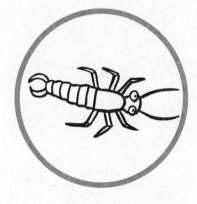

_arwig

_eacock

_abbit

Pesky Pests

Complete the crossword puzzle.

1. This winged insect can chew holes in clothing.
2. An insect that eats wood, even houses!
3. This insect leaves an itchy bite.
4. This scavenger searches for food at night.
5. You wouldn't want this bug in your bed!

Bird Word Search

Circle these words in the puzzle.

kingfisher

ostrich

peacock

puffin

pelican

kookaburra

parrot

```
K  I  N  G  F  I  S  H  E  R
P  S  D  E  V  T  Z  U  M  L
W  S  I  O  S  T  F  I  C  P
A  S  P  U  F  F  I  N  U  E
T  R  E  L  O  I  K  V  Y  L
X  P  A  R  R  O  T  I  O  L
A  W  C  T  G  V  N  K  J  I
K  O  O  K  A  B  U  R  R  A
Y  H  C  R  E  D  C  J  B  N
A  S  K  F  C  D  T  Y  U  I
X  C  Z  O  S  T  R  I  C  H
```

Amazing Plants

The raffia palm has the largest leaves in the world—they can grow as long as 80 ft. (24 m).

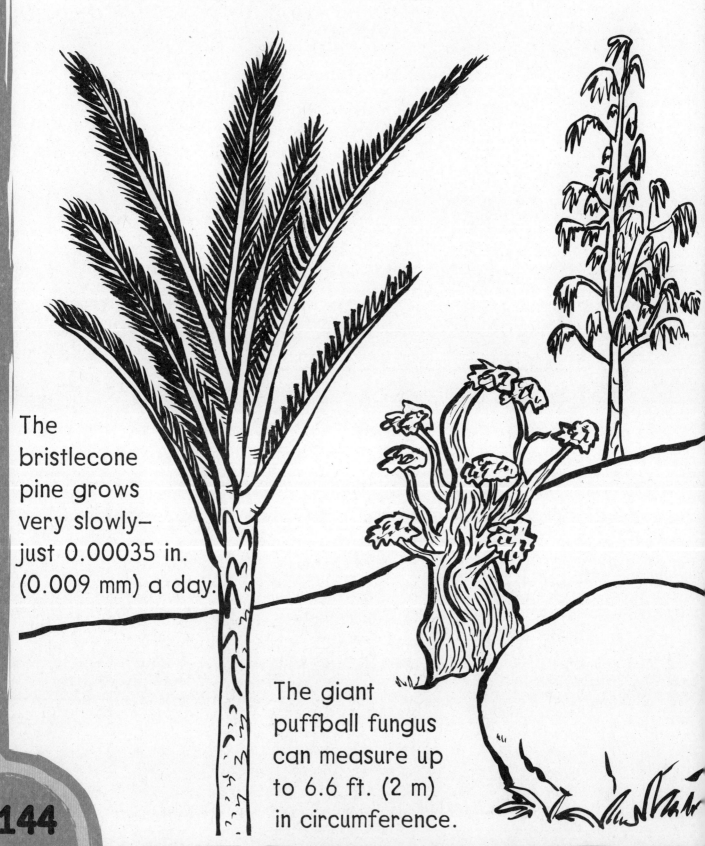

The bristlecone pine grows very slowly— just 0.00035 in. (0.009 mm) a day.

The giant puffball fungus can measure up to 6.6 ft. (2 m) in circumference.

Bamboo is the worlds fastest growing plant. It can grow 2 in. (5 cm) per hour.

A healthy, mature birch can produce up to 1 million seeds in a good year.

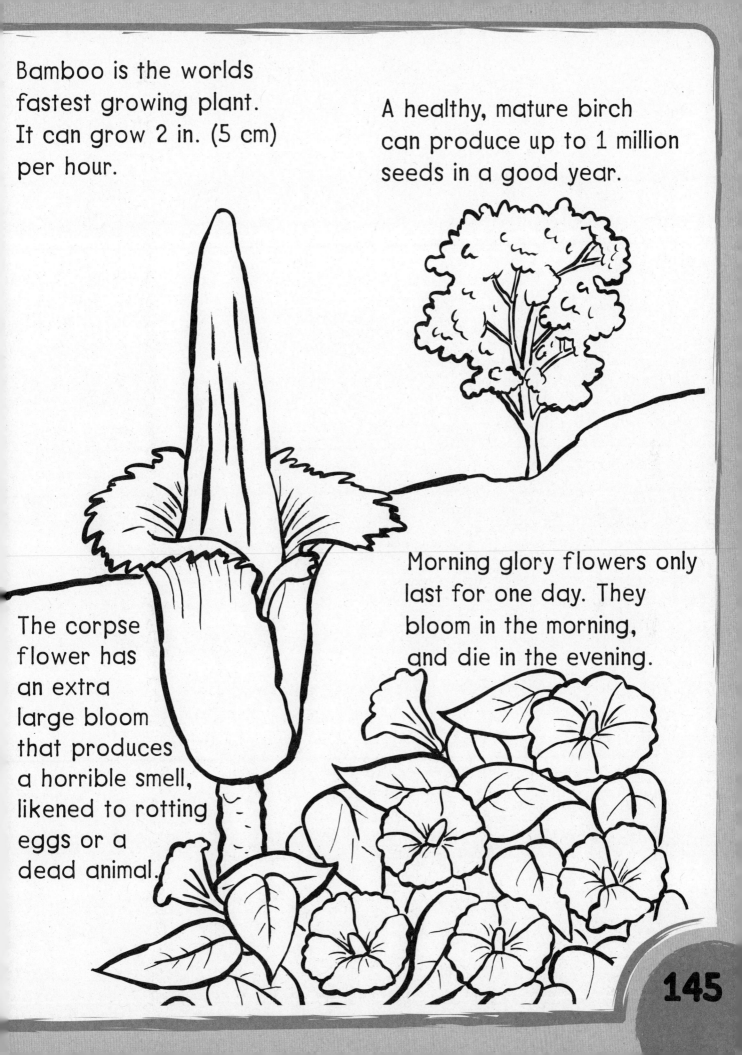

The corpse flower has an extra large bloom that produces a horrible smell, likened to rotting eggs or a dead animal.

Morning glory flowers only last for one day. They bloom in the morning, and die in the evening.

Tricky Traps

Which venus fly trap caught the fly?

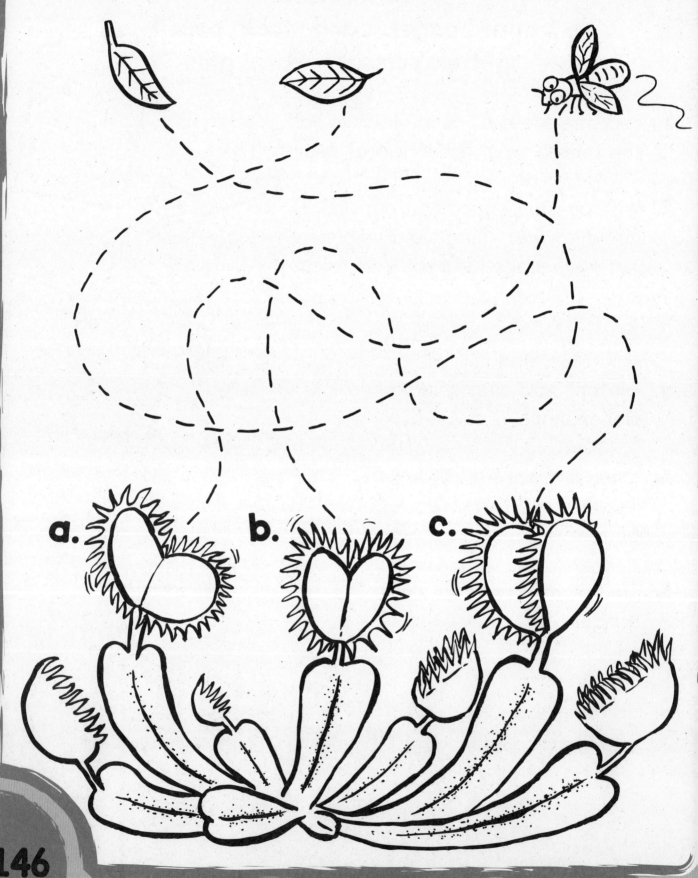

Make-and-Do Butterfly Mobile

You will need:
1 coat hanger, card stock, pencil glitter, scissors, yarn, glue

1. Fold the sheet of card stock in half. Along the folded side, draw half of a butterfly.

2. With an adult's help, cut out and unfold so that you have a whole butterfly shape. Repeat four times.

3. Cover the butterfly shapes with glue, and sprinkle glitter on top. Add sequins or other decorations, if desired.

4. Once dry, tape a different length of yarn onto each butterfly.

5. Tie the yarn onto the coat hanger.

Nature Detective

Find four different types of leaves outside.

Draw a picture of each leaf in a box.
Can you name the tree that each leaf came from?

_____

_____

Perched

Color the picture.

Number Problems

Complete the addition and subtraction problems.

12	+	4	=	
-	■	+	■	-
10	-		=	8
=	■	=	■	=
2	+	6	=	

	-	16	=	3
+	■	-	■	+
2	+		=	14
=	■	=	■	=
21	-	4	=	

Slippery Snake

An anaconda can grow up to 26 ft. (8 m) long.
What has this anaconda swallowed?

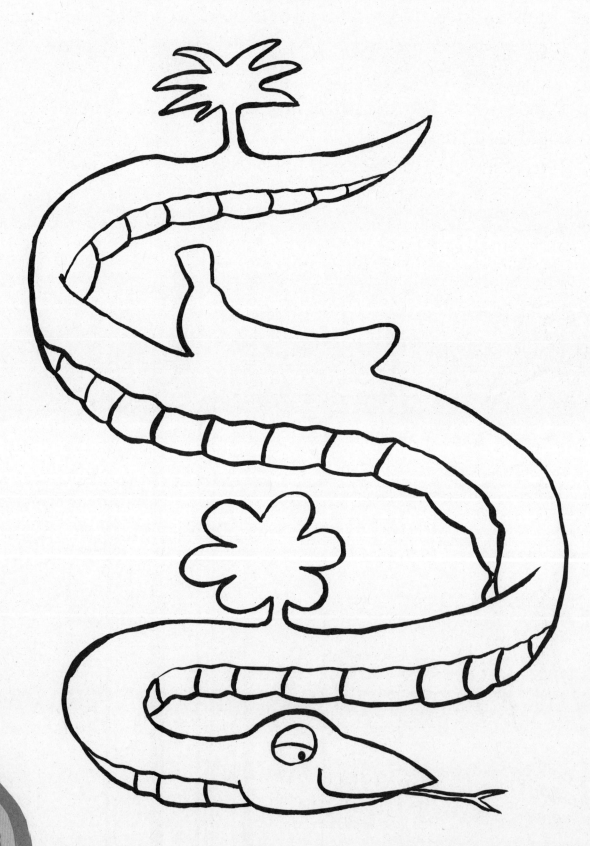

Wise Owls

Complete the crossword puzzle.

1. I get my name from a farmyard building where I may be found
2. I get my name from one of the largest birds of prey
3. My name is the opposite of *greater*
4. I have white feathers and my name is also a type of cold weather
5. I have mottled brown feathers

Hidden Nature

Color this picture.

What Can You See?

Take a walk with an adult and see what plants and animals you can find.
Circle something...

stripy   blue   brown and furry

spiky   green and soft

F-ant-astic

Draw a line to help the ant return to its colony.

Start

Finish

Number Word Search

Complete the addition and subtraction problems.
Circle the missing number words in the word search.

10 - ☐ = 5   10 + 6 = ☐

5 + 4 = ☐   8 + 4 = ☐

8 - 4 = ☐   6 - 3 = ☐

S	N	S	P	X	N	R	E
T	H	R	E	E	P	I	F
O	F	U	W	R	T	H	O
D	I	R	E	J	W	S	U
O	V	R	T	S	E	C	R
D	E	E	L	Y	L	N	P
R	F	N	X	H	V	I	M
S	I	X	T	E	E	N	L
K	M	C	O	C	A	E	K

Number Keys

Use the key to solve the addition
and subtraction problems.

Key

2	4	6	8	10

 + = ☐

 −  = ☐

 +  = ☐

 − = ☐

159

Feeding Time

Color the picture.

160

Under Cover

Insects often hide under things where it is dark,
damp, cool, and safe from predators.
What might you find under these objects?
A rock?   A fallen branch?   Some leaves?

Butterfly Beauty

Color the picture.

Number Word Search

Complete the addition and subtraction problems.
Circle the answers in the word search.

6 + 6 = ☐   10 + 8 = ☐

7 + 4 = ☐   5 + 5 = ☐

4 + 5 = ☐   10 + 10 = ☐

```
Z I O H N I N E
T E N E B P I I
W N U W R T W G
E E R E J W S H
N R R L S E H T
T V E E Y L N E
Y F N V H V I E
S T W E L V E N
K M C N C A E K
```

Brilliant Beetles

Circle the words in the puzzle.

jewel

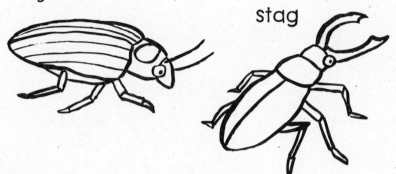

stag

dung

scarab

tiger

weevil

```
Z L W E E V I L
D B E V T L S J
U E U W I T C E
N Y R E G W A W
G T R L E E R E
T L E E R L A L
Y E N V H V B R
S T A G L V E D
K B A E T L E K
```

Monkey Message

Unscramble the letters to discover what these monkeys are saying to each other.

I tanw a aannba

"

__ __ __ __ __ __ .

Em oto

"

__ __ __ __ __ .

Fantastic Insects

An orb-weaver spider makes a copy of itself to fool birds into eating the fake spider.

Insect farms encourage farmers to use certain insects as natural pesticides, because they eat crop-destroying bugs.

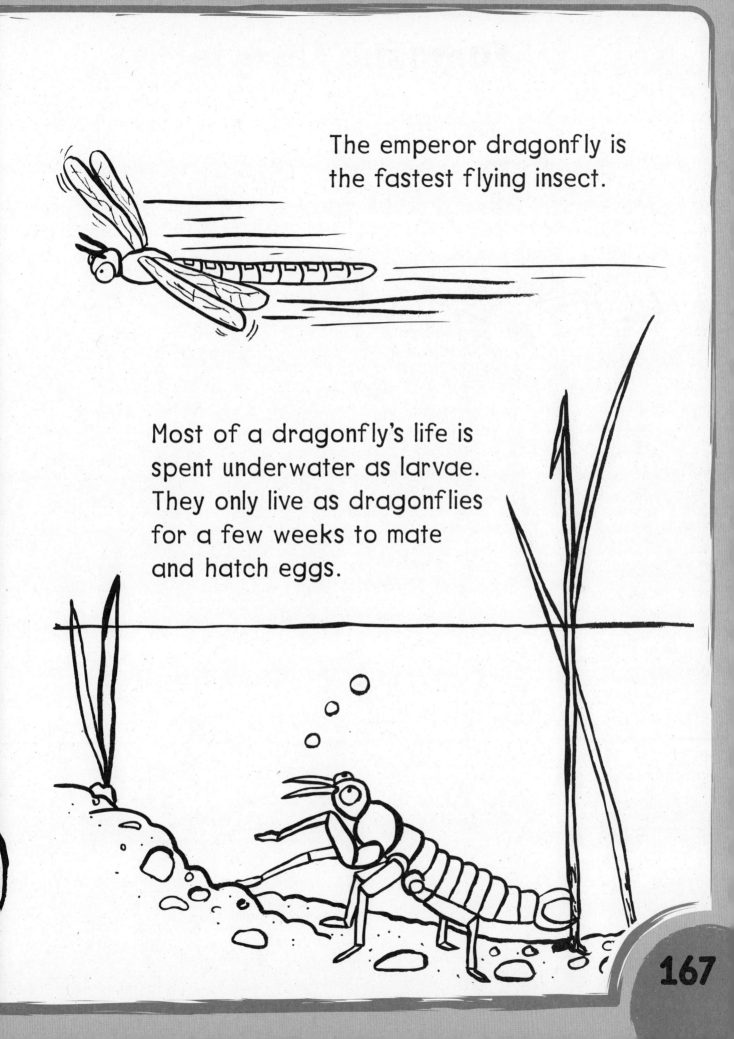

The emperor dragonfly is the fastest flying insect.

Most of a dragonfly's life is spent underwater as larvae. They only live as dragonflies for a few weeks to mate and hatch eggs.

Make-and-Do Miss Cress

You will need: **skin-colored tights, scissors, cress seed, marker, sawdust, googly eyes, glue, plant pot**

1. Ask permission to use an old pair of tights.

2. With adult help, cut the top section off of one of the legs and fill the foot end with cress seeds. Then, fill the rest with sawdust.

3. Tie the open end in a knot.

4. Draw a face with a marker, or glue googly eyes and other items to make a face.

5. Place in a flowerpot, and lightly water. Watch her hair grow!

Earthworm Mischief

Measure each earthworm.
Which earthworm is longest?

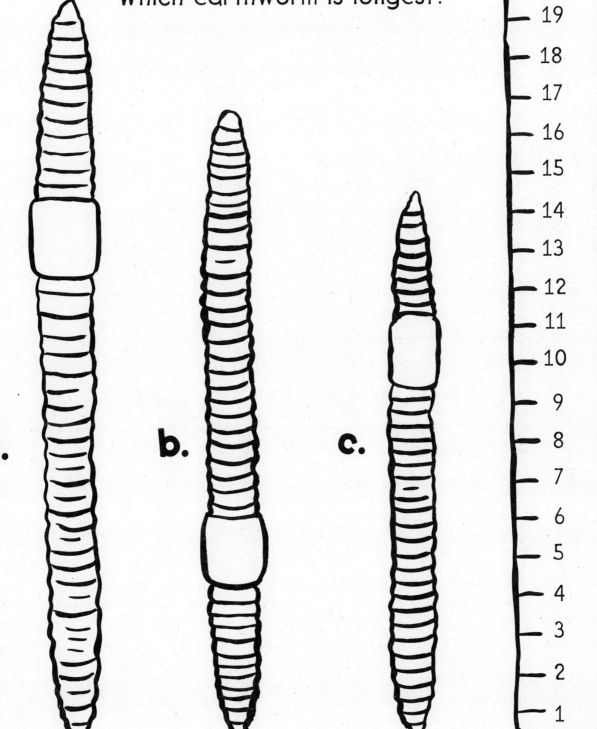

a.

b.

c.

20
19
18
17
16
15
14
13
12
11
10
9
8
7
6
5
4
3
2
1

Did you know that sunlight is fatal to the earthworm?
It has no protection from the sun's strong rays.

Rocking Robin

Color the picture.

Number Word Search

Complete the addition and subtraction problems.
Circle the missing number words in the puzzle.

12 + 3 = ☐   5 + ☐ = 9

☐ + 3 = 5   10 + 3 = ☐

2 + 5 = ☐   4 + 4 = ☐

```
E  I  G  H  T  S  P  T
O  I  R  V  I  T  A  W
R  B  X  P  U  H  R  O
A  F  O  C  R  I  R  S
Y  O  G  L  T  R  O  E
E  U  E  E  A  T  T  V
E  R  R  M  T  E  J  E
L  F  I  F  T  E  E  N
A  R  T  Y  C  N  P  D
```

Snappy Word Search

Circle these words in the puzzle.

TEETH SNOUT CLAWS SCALES TAIL

CAIMAN ALLIGATOR CROCODILE

```
E U T X M X A C
O I A V I S L R
C A I M A N L O
L F L H R O I C
A F S L T U G O
W R L E A T A D
S T E E T H T I
L F S F T E O L
S C A L E S R E
```

Find the Difference

Circle the differences in the pictures.

Park Puzzle

Help these travellers tour this national park and return to base camp.

Start

What do they see on the way?

Finish

Number Crossword

Complete the addition problems and write the
answers in the crossword.

↓1. 6 + 5 = ☐   3. 9 + 7 = ☐

1. 3 + 5 = ☐   4. 9 + 3 = ☐
→

2. 19 + 1 = ☐   5. 5 + 4 = ☐

Berry Sweet Treats

Bright, colorful berries are easier for birds to find.
Draw some berries on this bush.

All Mixed-Up

Can you identify all of the animals shown below?
What would you call this odd creature?

Word Search

Circle these words in the puzzle.

cassowary

kiwi

kakapo

penguin

ostrich

emu

M	U	X	X	M	L	P	C
L	O	R	V	I	K	A	A
P	E	N	G	U	I	N	S
A	M	G	E	L	W	R	S
Y	U	G	K	Y	I	O	O
E	R	E	E	A	O	T	W
O	S	T	R	I	C	H	A
L	E	I	C	L	O	W	R
K	A	K	A	P	O	E	Y

Spinning Spider

Color the picture.

Trusty Trees

How many things can you think of that are made from trees? Draw them in this box.

Did you know that it takes approximately 2 tons of timber to make 1 ton of paper?

Number Crossword

Complete the addition and subtraction problems.
Write the answers in the crossword.

1. 15 − 2 = ☐   **4.** 2 + 3 = ☐

2. 10 + 2 = ☐   **5.** 4 + 4 = ☐

3. 25 − 6 = ☐   **6.** 9 + 5 = ☐

Pretty Petals

Draw more petals so that all of the flowers have the same number of petals.

Tree Dwellers

Ayes-ayes have an extra long middle finger, which they use to dig insects from tree holes.

Bushbabies have long legs for leaping and large eyes, which help them see in the dark. Their name comes from the sound that they make, which is like a crying baby.

Animals climb trees to escape predators, and to eat fruit and leaves.

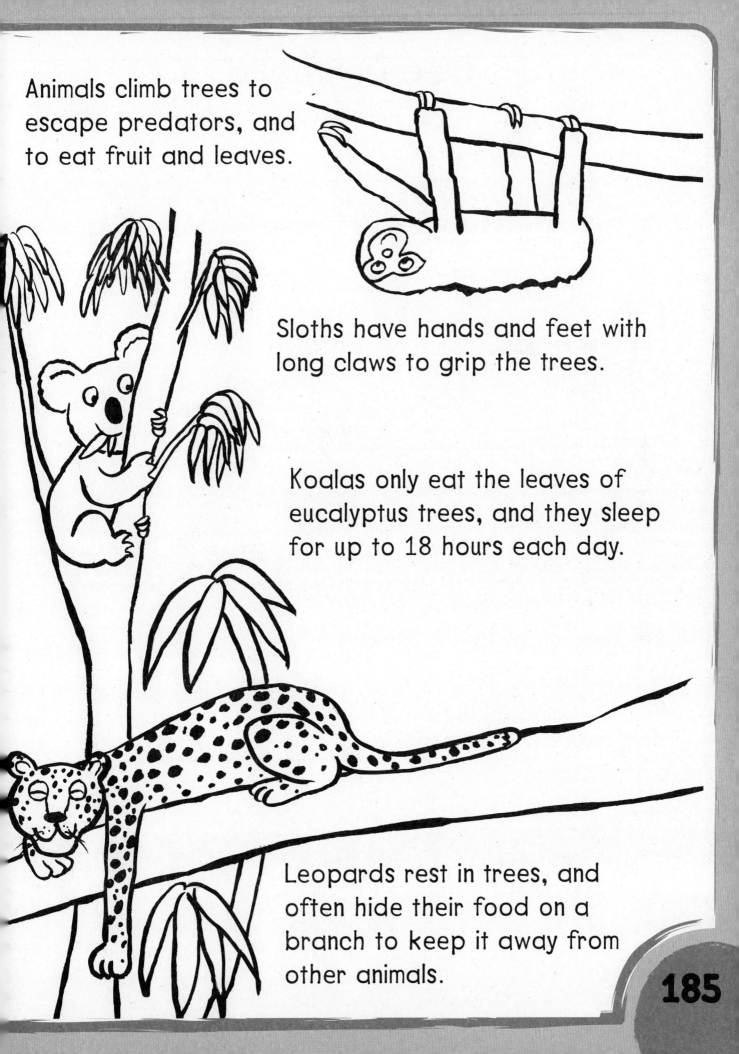

Sloths have hands and feet with long claws to grip the trees.

Koalas only eat the leaves of eucalyptus trees, and they sleep for up to 18 hours each day.

Leopards rest in trees, and often hide their food on a branch to keep it away from other animals.

Find the Difference

Circle the differences in the pictures.

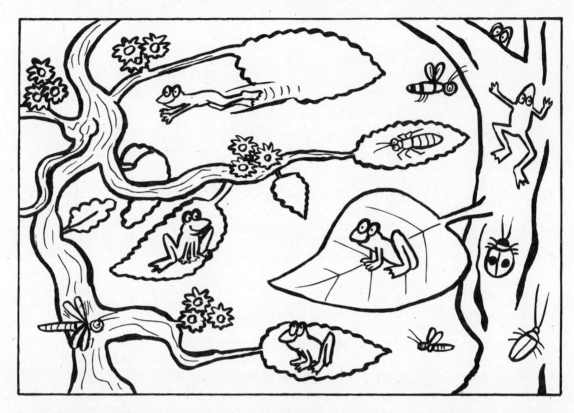

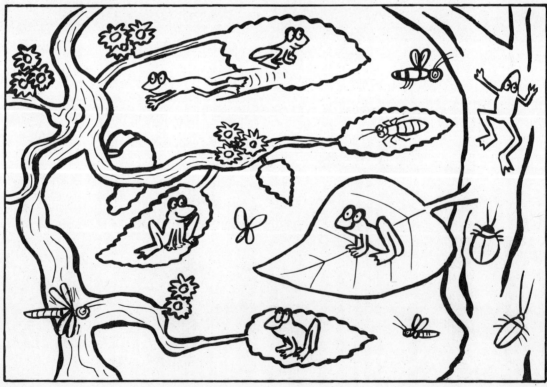

Number Crossword

Complete the addition and subtraction problems.
Write the answers in the crossword.

1. 12 + 8 = ☐   **4.** 5 + 4 = ☐

2. 10 − 7 = ☐   **5.** 3 + 3 = ☐

3. 12 − 1 = ☐   **6.** 11 + 5 = ☐

Word Muddle

Unscramble these letters to discover
the names of two insects.

yBetnetrilpCfetdue

_ _ _ _ _ _ _ _ _

_ _ _ _ _ _ _ _

Burrow Business

Draw a line to help the rabbit return to its burrow.

Start

Finish

189

Snake Family

Color the picture.

Flying Bugs

Circle these words in the puzzle.

 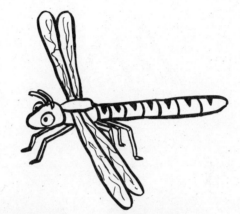

DRAGONFLY   **LACEWING**   **MOTH**

WASP   **HONEYBEE**

```
L  D  T  X  M  L  H  H
A  R  R  V  I  G  O  B
C  A  D  Y  U  G  N  W
E  G  R  D  L  T  E  D
W  O  G  L  Y  A  Y  L
I  N  M  O  T  H  B  I
N  F  R  R  T  P  E  M
G  L  S  L  A  C  E  N
T  Y  W  A  S  P  S  D
```

What Am I?

I make a buzzing noise.
I like hot weather.
I give an itchy bite.

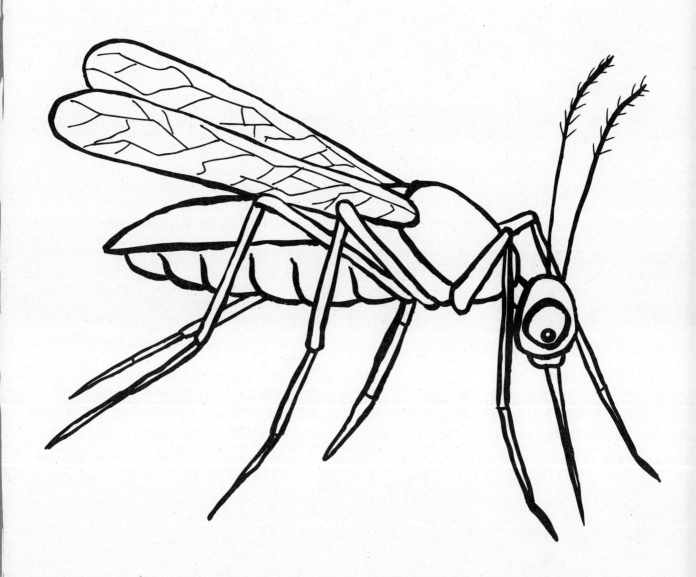

I am a _____ .

Tree Jumble

Unscramble the names of these tree-dwelling animals.

quaecaM

_____

ugtnnOraa

_____

wlerHo
nomyek

_____

_____

ianDa keynom

_____

yeA-aey

_____

bobinG

_____

IdGoen nsub
onsed mynoke

_____

_____

loSht

____

Trace the Tracks

Which animal ate the flowers in the garden?
Identify the animal tracks to find the culprit.

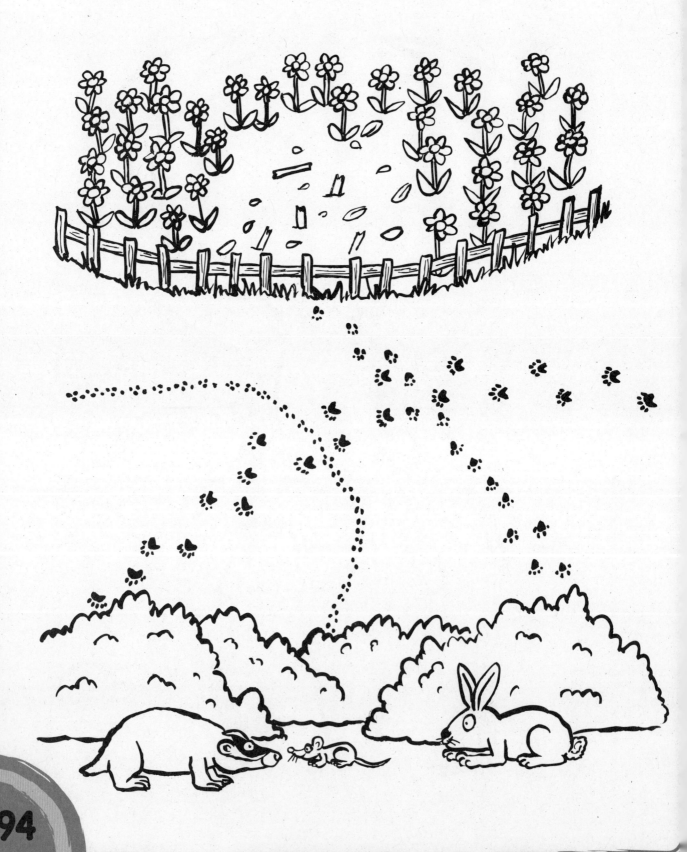

Stinger Vision

A scorpion can have up to 12 eyes.
Draw eyes on this scorpion.

195

Beautiful Butterfly

Color the picture.

All Mixed-Up

Can you identify all of the animals shown below?
What would you call this odd creature?

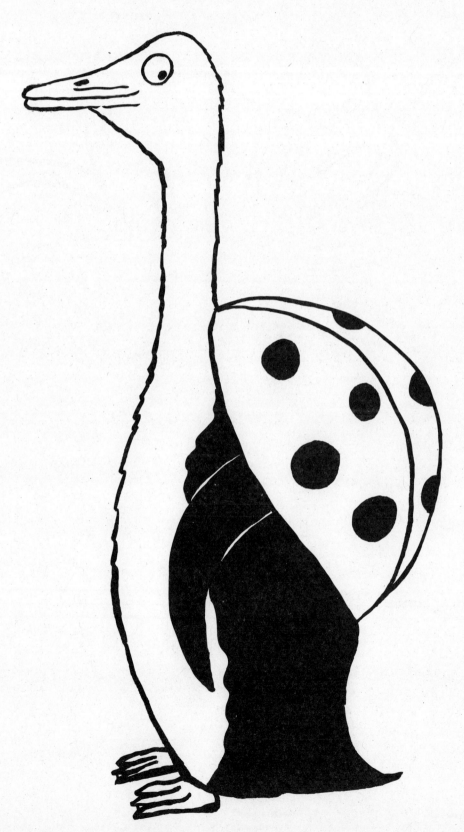

Bird Word Search

Circle these words in the puzzle.

seagull

toucan

stork

swan

woodpecker

vulture

```
W O O D P E C K E R
M U T X M L S N I D
S O G D S E T S E R
E T C P E R O S T K
S A N G A A R W P L
Y A G L G A K A L E
E R T O U C A N S N
E O R R L P E O J F
U E I C L R W N V D
V U L T U R E A C M
```

Lovely Leaf

Draw the leaf in the grid.

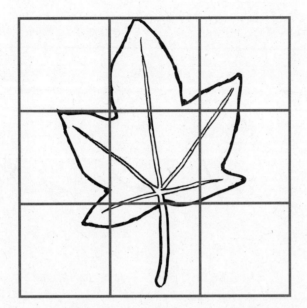

Monkey Facts

Diana monkeys, like hamsters, have cheek pouches to store food.

Monkeys belong to a group of animals called primates. Lemurs, apes, and humans are all primates.

Most primates are good at climbing and can grip using their fingers, toes, and tails.

Howler monkeys are one of the loudest land animals.
They can be heard up to 3 miles (5 km) away.

Cotton top monkeys
are among the
smallest monkeys.

Orangutans are the
largest tree-dwelling
mammals in the world.

Winged Words

Use the key to solve the message below.

" __ __ __

__ __ __ __ __

__ __ __ __ __

__ __ __ __ __ __ -

"

__ __ __ .

A B C D

E F G H

I J K L

M N O P

Q R S T

U V W Y Z

Number Problems

Complete the addition and subtraction problems.

8	**+**		**=**	**10**
+	■	**−**	■	**+**
8	**−**	**2**	**=**	
=	■	**=**	■	**=**
	+	**0**	**=**	

5	**+**	**6**	**=**	
+	■	**−**	■	**+**
4	**−**		**=**	**1**
=	■	**=**	■	**=**
	+	**3**	**=**	

Design Time

Design your own animal. Think about its diet, its camouflage, and how it adapts to its environment. Name your animal.

Deep Trouble

Draw a line to help the badger return to its burrow.

Start

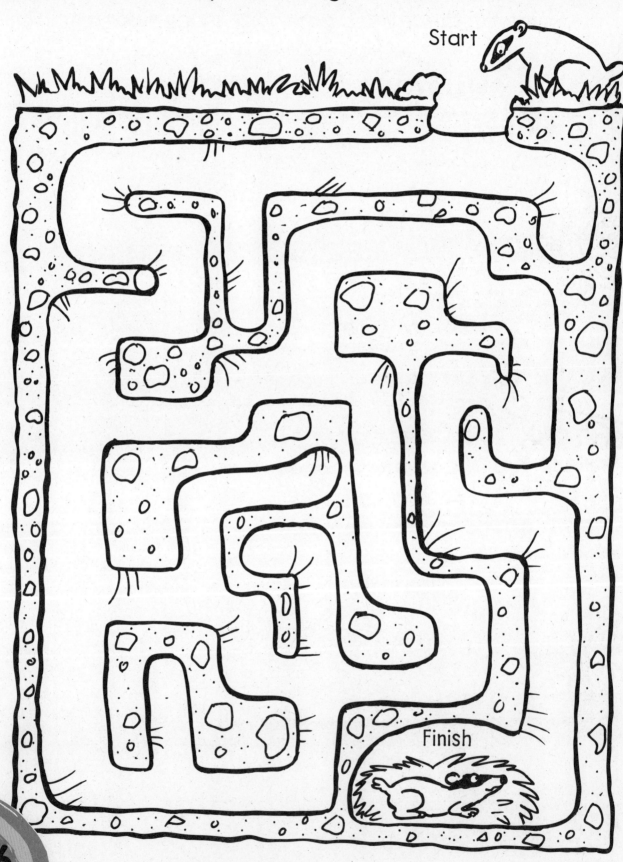

Finish

206

Butterfly Brilliance

Fit these butterfly names into the crossword.
Some of the letters have been done for you.

SWALLOWTAIL   **FRITILLARY**

SKIPPER   **ADMIRAL**   **HOLLY BLUE**

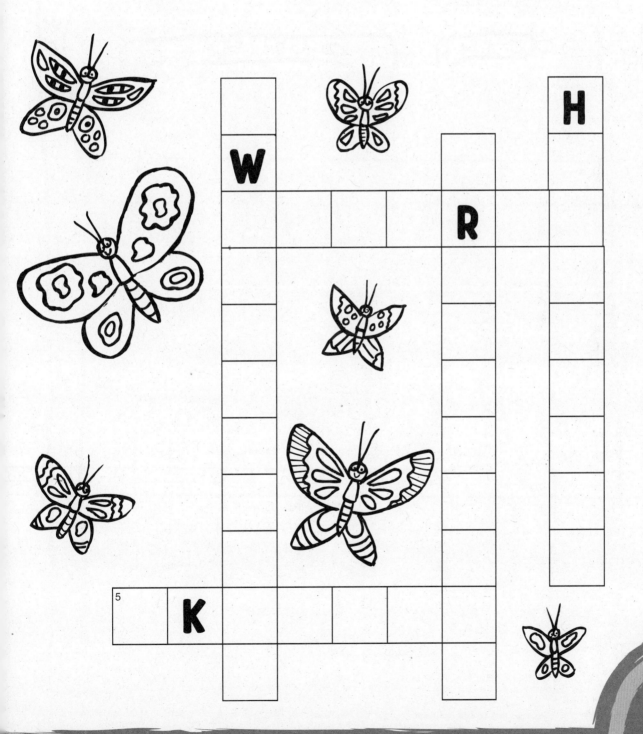

Bright and Beautiful

The male blue morpho butterfly can have a wingspan
of 8 in. (20 cm), and has a very bright appearance.
Color this picture.

Snail Trail

Which snail doesn't belong?

a.

b.
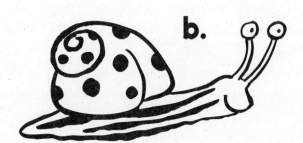

c.

d.

e.

f.

Berry Merry Birds

Color the picture.

Which Is the Tallest?

The record for the tallest sunflower is 25 ft. 5 in. (7.76 m). Which of these sunflowers is the tallest?

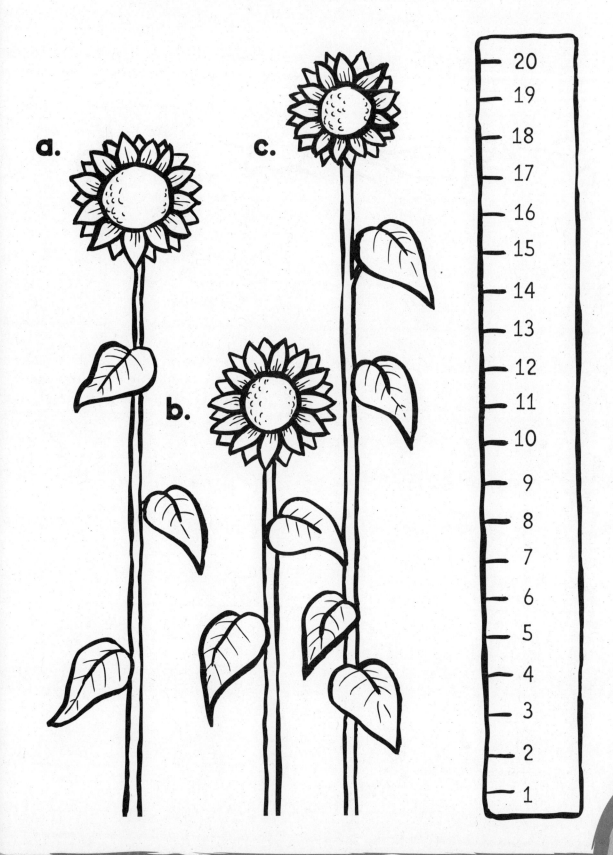

Underwater Trees

Seaweed is a useful hiding place for small fish.
How many fish can you find? _____

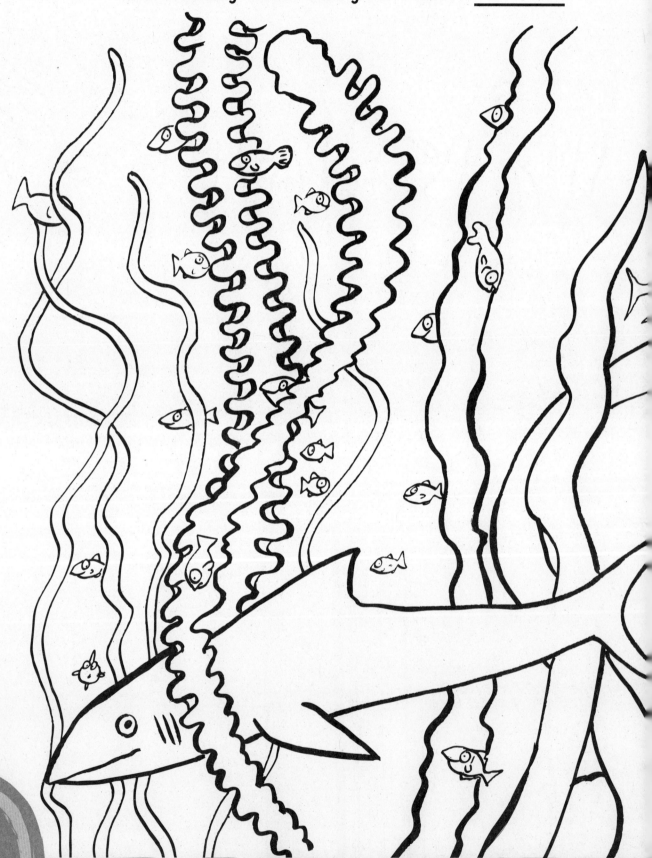

Trowel Trail

The gardener has lost her trowel.
Help her through the maze to find it.

Start

Finish

Secret Shadows

What types of flowers made these shadows?

a.

_ _ _ _ _ _ _ _

b.

_ _ _ _ _

c.

_ _ _ _ _

d.

_ _ _ _

Tongue Twister

These frogs' tongues are twisted together.
Which frog caught the fly?

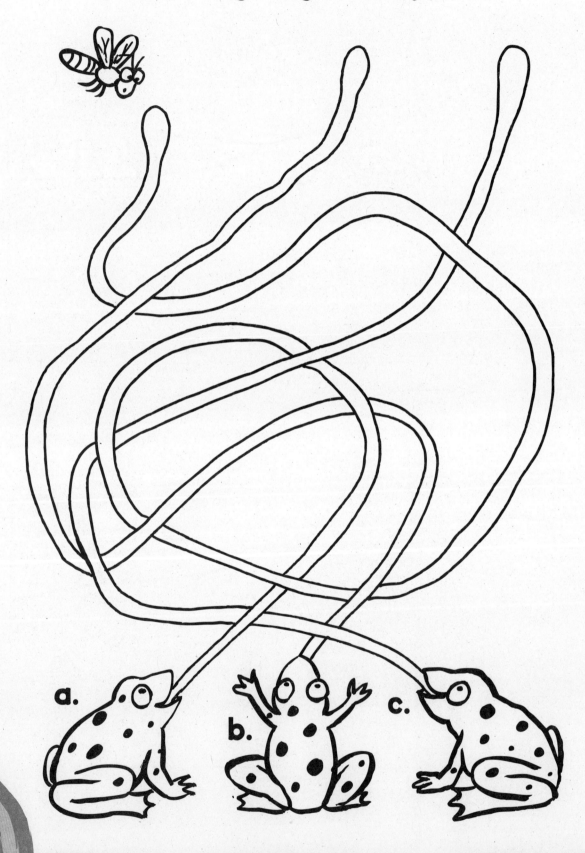

Find the Difference

Circle the differences in the pictures.

Find the Difference

Circle the differences in the pictures.

Hollow Homes

Animals often make homes in old, hollowed-out trees, because they provide shelter and protection. How many squirrels can you find in this tree? _____

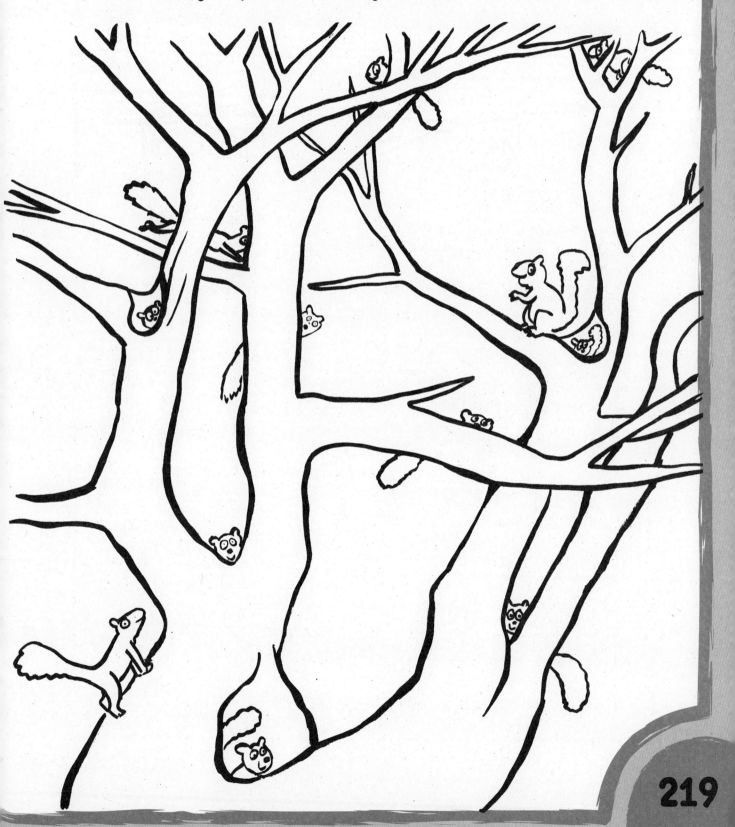

Hide Away

Color the picture.

Copy Cat

Draw the toucan in the grid.

The Beetles

Draw a line to match each pair of beetles.

1.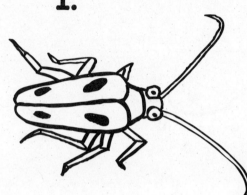

a.

2.

b.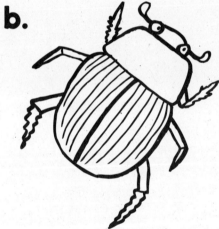

3.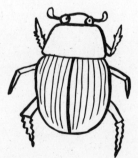

c.

Leaf Likeness

Draw a line to match each pair of leaves.

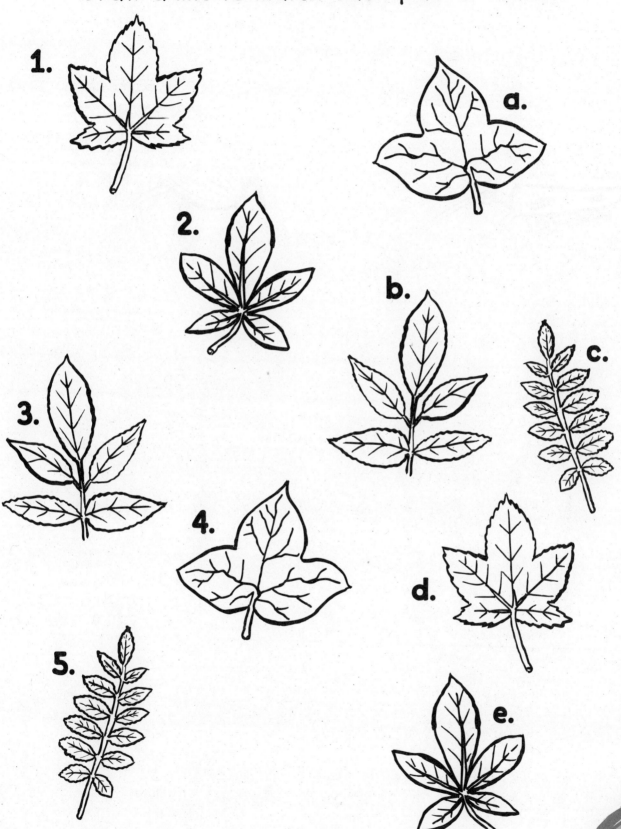

1.

2.

3.

4.

5.

a.

b.

c.

d.

e.

At Home

Circle the things in this picture that could harm the environment.

Did you know that if a single faucet drips once every minute, it wastes 34 gallons of water each year?

Amazon Adventure

Imagine you've been on a trip to the Amazon.
Draw pictures of what you would expect to see.

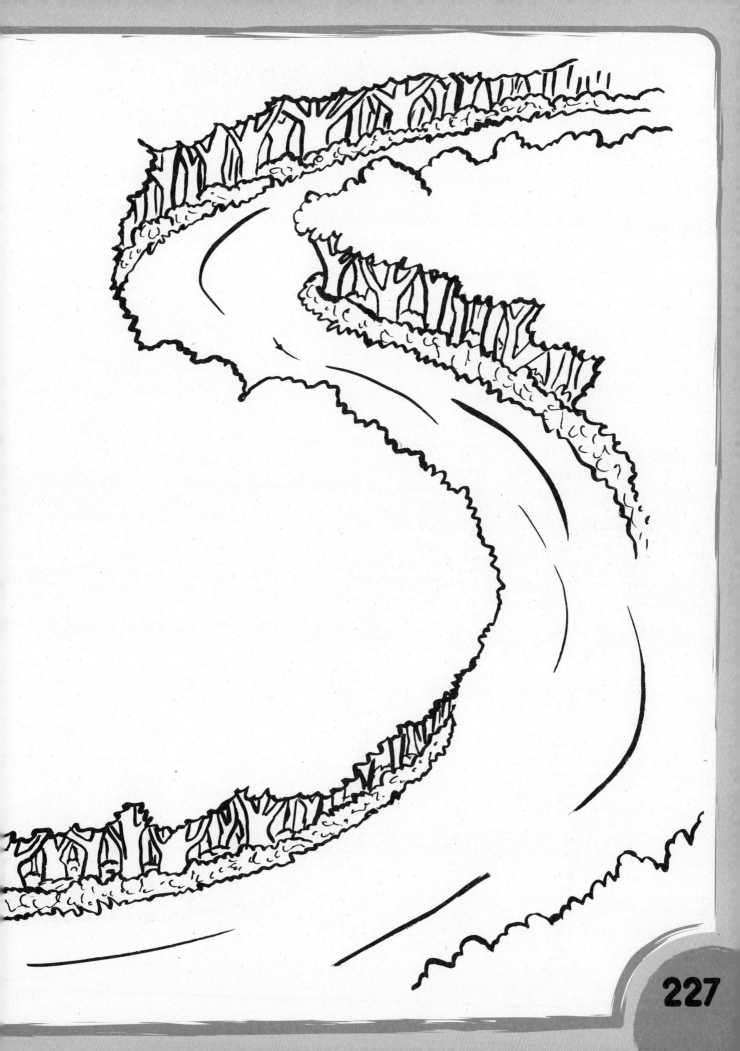

227

Trivia Time

The Amazon rain forest in South America is twice the size of which country?

a. England

b. Russia

c. India

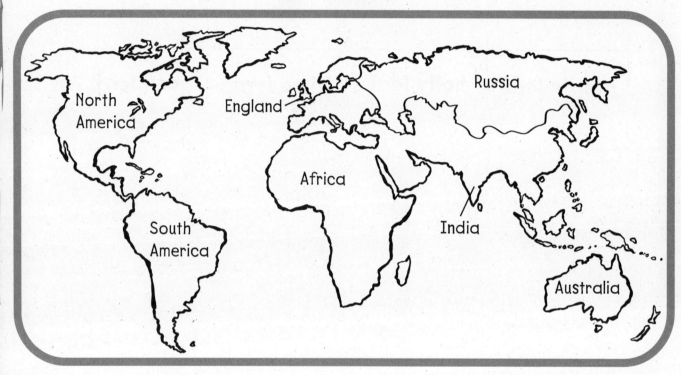

How many orchid seeds would fill a tablespoon?

a. 25

b. 250

c. 25,000

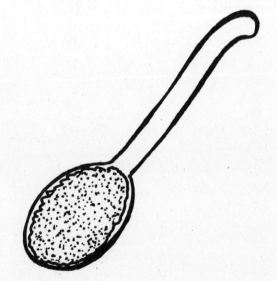

Number Keys

Use the key to solve these number problems.

maple leaf	holly leaf	lime leaf	ash leaf
4	5	6	7

Hood's Hideout

Sherwood Forest is known for the legend of Robin Hood.
Can you see him hiding in this scene?

Roadrunner Race

Solve the number problems to see which roadrunner is the fastest. The lowest total wins.

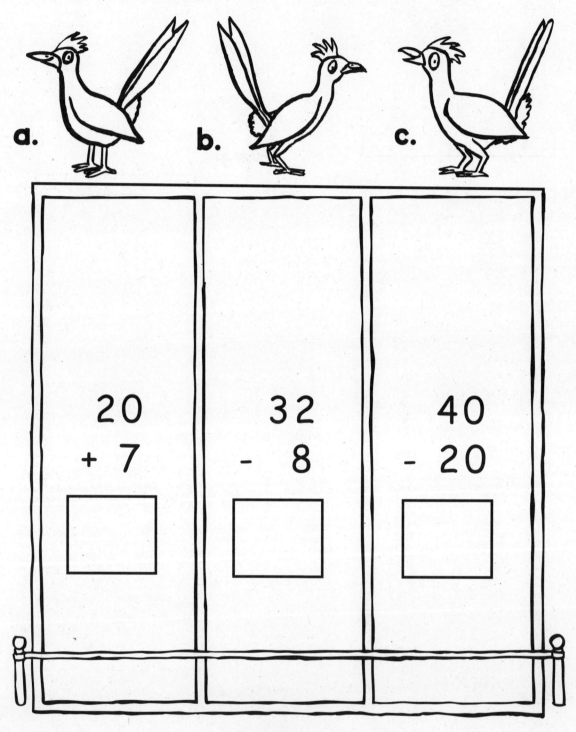

a.

b.

c.

$$20 + 7$$

$$32 - 8$$

$$40 - 20$$

Answers

Pages 2-3
7 animals

Page 6

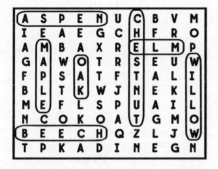

Page 12

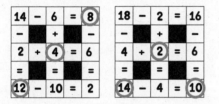

Page 15

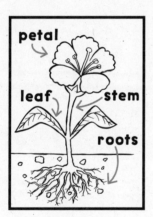

Page 16
d.

Page 17

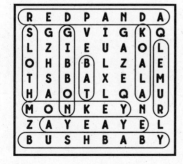

Page 24
Monkey Tree

Page 25
22 legs

Pages 26-27
11 birds

Page 29
10 worms

Page 30
a.; a.

Page 31
The disappearance of bees in the US is a mystery.

Page 33

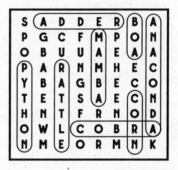

Page 34
5 goats

Page 35
d.

Page 36

Page 37
Fly

Page 40
a.

233

Answers

Page 41

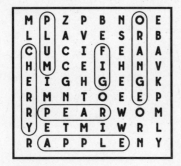

Word search grid (Page 41):
```
H K M M I N G P A
B I T D F G T R L
R D P P I G A A B
A O F E N T O R A
Y V K L C A R R T
D E U E H O T O R
E O R I N E A T O
L Z E A G L E H S
C A N A R Y P S
```
Circled words: DOVE, FINCH, PARROT, ALBATROS(S), EAGLE, CANARY

Pages 42-43

18 flowers

Page 44

In the rainforest, most **plant** and **animal** life is not found on the **forest** floor, but in the leafy world known as the canopy. The **canopy**, which may be more than 100 feet above the ground, is made up of the overlapping branches and **leaves** in the **trees**.

Page 45

Bee, sea, flea, me, glee, key, free, knee, pea, see, fee, he, she. Can you think of any more?

Page 48

Word search grid (Page 48):
```
S R S P L N B E
L E A V E S F B
C O C I F E R A
D A R I I H U V
O G N E T B I K
E R N T B E T P
V E N T B U D S
E E T M I W C L
R B A R K S N Z
```
Circled words: LEAVES, FRUIT, ACORN, FIR, BUDS, BARK

Page 49

Tapir

Page 51

Monkey

Page 53

Rose, daisy, iris, poppy, daffodil, carnation, heather, lily, lilac, tulip, sweet pea, sunflower, freesia, begonia, and honeysuckle. Can you think of any more?

Page 54

Word search grid (Page 54):
```
M P Z P B N O E
L L A V E S R B
C U C F I F A A
H M I I G H N V
E I G G T O G K
R M N T O E E P
R P E A R W O M
Y E T M I W R L
R A P P L E N Y
```
Circled words: PLUM, FIG, ORANGE, CHERRY, PEAR, APPLE

Page 55

Cheese

Page 60

Crossword (Page 60): bluebird, nightingale, starling, chaffinch

Page 64

It's a trick question—they all can!

Page 65

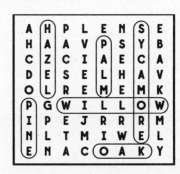

Word search grid (Page 65):
```
A H P L E N S S E
H A A V E S Y B
C Z C I P E C A
D E S E A H A V
O L R M L E M K
P G W I L L O W
I E J R R R E M
N P T M I W E L
E N A C O A K Y
```
Circled words: HAZEL, PALM, SYCAMORE, WILLOW, PINE, OAK

Page 66

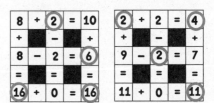

Math grids (Page 66):

Grid 1:
8	+	②	=	10
+		−		+
8	−	2	=	⑥
=		=		=
⑯	+	0	=	⑯

Grid 2:
②	+	2	=	④
+		−		+
9	−	②	=	7
=		=		=
11	+	0	=	⑪

Page 67

234

Answers

Page 68

Page 69

Page 71

```
          h
      f   o
      l   n
  P o l l e n
      w   y
      d r o n e
          e
          c
          t
          a
          r
```

Pages 72-73

I live in a colony. I have six legs; ant.

Pages 74-75

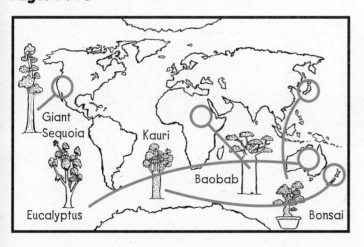

Page 76

Stick bug

Page 78

d.

Page 84

A butterfly, an ant, and a monkey

Page 85

9 dragonflies

Page 86

Brazil; Bolivia; Indonesia; Congo; Angola; Venezuela; Papua New Guinea; Mexico; India.

Page 87

b.; a.

Page 88

Page 89

Pages 90-91

4 flies; 4 wasps; 5 grubs; 5 beetles; and 4 caterpillars

Page 93

Grub

Page 95

```
              t
      d       a
      r       d
  t o a d     p
      g       o
      o       l
  p o n d w e e d
      f
  l i l y
```

Answers

Page 96
Leaves; wood; trunk; soil; bark; branch; sunlight; fruit; seed; sap; roots; and water

Page 101

④	+	9	=	13		⑤	+	11	=	16
+				−		+		+		+
10	−	③	=	7		6	+	③	=	9
=				=		=		=		=
14	+	6	=	㉑		11	+	14	=	㉕

Page 102
Leaf

Page 103

```
l               k
o               e
r     m a c a w
i               c
k               k
e               a
budgerigar
t               o
                o
```

Page 104

```
S  P H L E N S E
P (H O W L E R) R
I  N W I M B E M
D (G Z L P H A A
E  I R E X M O C
R  B W I Z R O A
S  B A C L P E Q
 (C O L O B U S) U
P  N A C Z U E  E
```

Page 106
c

Page 107
b

Page 108
a. 7; b. 10; c. 12; d. 16

Page 109

Page 111
c.

Page 112

```
        t
        o
        u
  c     c
m a c a w
  s     n
  s
  o
  w
  a
l o r i k e e t
  y
h o r n b i l l
  y
```

Page 113
b. and h.

Page 116
A dragonfly, a ladybug, and a spider.

Page 117
Acorn

Page 121
Spied, pie, dry, ride, sail, pail, ripe, pear, leap, seal, dial, sales, spread, repays, lily, pillars, sadly, lady, drapes, rapidly, spires, players, rasped, reads, parsley, spells, and silly. Can you think of any more?

Page 124
"Pretty Polly wants a cracker."

Page 126

```
B L P L E T S E
S(F I V E)W Y E B
C O H I A E Y F A
D U Z E L L I F V
O(S R E M)V I T E
Q(E L E V E N)W N
I V T A R R E O L
F(E I G H T)L L Y
E N A C O A N Y
```

Page 127

```
H P H L E N M E
(S N A I L)C I R
C N W I M X L J
D G Z L P A L A
(W O R M)E O P C
P J N W Z R P F
(F L Y)A L P G U
C O L A S P E E
P N A P(B E E)S
```

236

Answers

Page 128

d.

Page 129

b.; c.

Page 132

10 bees

Page 133

Wasp

Page 136

31 acorns

Page 137

a.

Page 138

```
H  P  T  L  E  N  M  E  C  V
B  L  A  C  K  W  I  D  O  W
P  N  R  W  I  O  E  Q  L  D
U  G  A  E  M  L  K  X  V  Z
R  E  N  B  P  F  L  L  O  X
S  B  T  W  B  R  S  F  N  E
E  L  U  A  S  P  I  G  E  R
C  O  L  L  S  E  D  E  B  H
P  M  A  M  O  N  E  Y  S  P
```

Page 141

Iguana; scorpion; dragonfly; earwig; peacock; rabbit.

Page 142

```
      m o t h
    m     e
  c o c k r o a c h
    s     m
    q     i
    u     t
    i     8 b e d b u g
    t
    o
```

Page 143

```
K  I  N  G  F  I  S  H  E  R
P  S  D  E  V  T  Z  U  M  L
W  S  I  O  S  T  F  I  C  P
A  T  P  U  F  F  I  N  U  E
T  R  E  L  O  I  K  V  F  L
X  P  A  R  R  O  T  I  O  I
A  W  C  T  G  V  L  K  J  C
K  O  O  K  A  B  U  R  R  A
Y  H  C  R  F  D  C  J  B  N
A  S  K  F  C  D  T  Y  U  I
X  C  Z  O  S  T  R  I  C  H
```

Page 146

a.

Page 151

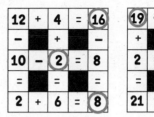

Page 152

A palm tree, a banana, and a flower.

Page 153

Page 157

Page 158

```
S  N  L  P  X  N  R  E
T  H  R  E  E  P  I  F
O  D  F  U  W  R  H  O
O  O  I  R  E  T  S  U
D  R  V  E  T  S  C  R
R  F  E  N  X  H  N  P
S  I  X  T  E  E  N  L
K  M  C  O  C  A  E  K
```

237

Answers

Page 159

2 + 10 = 12; 8 - 4 = 4; 10 + 6 = 16; 4 - 2 = 2

Page 163

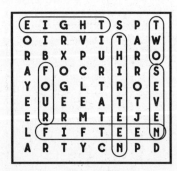

Page 164

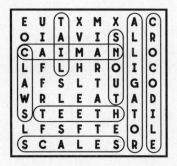

Page 165

"I want a banana.", "Me too!"

Page 169

a.

Page 171

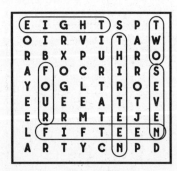

Page 172

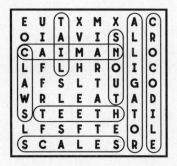

Pages 173

Pages 174–175

Page 176

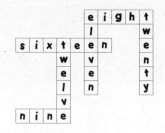

Page 178

A goat, a bear, and a lemur.

Page 179

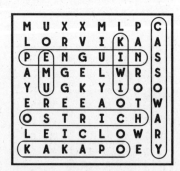

Page 182

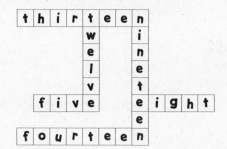

238

Answers

Page 186

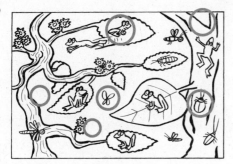

Page 187

Page 188

Butterfly; centipede

Page 189

Page 191

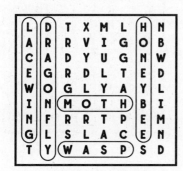

Page 192

Mosquito

Page 193

Howler monkey; Macaque; Orangutan; Diana monkey; Aye-aye; Gibbon; Golden snub-nosed monkey; Sloth.

Page 194

Rabbit

Page 197

An emu, a ladybug, and a penguin.

Page 198

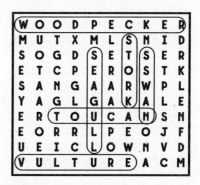

Pages 202-203

"I am going to be a butterfly."

Page 204

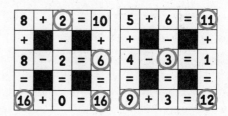

Page 206

Page 207

Answers

Page 209

e.

Page 211

c.

Pages 212-213

37 fish

Page 214

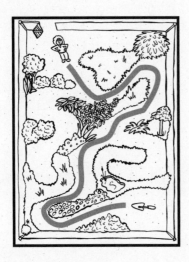

Page 215

a. daffodil; b. daisy; c. tulip; d. rose

Page 216

a.

Page 217

Page 218

Page 219

12 squirrels

Page 222

1-c; 2-a; 3-b

Page 223

1-d; 2-e; 3-b; 4-a; 5-c.

Pages 224-225

Page 228

c.; c.

Page 229

4+5=9; 6+7=13; 4+6=10; 5+7=12

Pages 230-231

Page 232

c.